I would like to thank the many organizations featured in this book for their co-operation and enthusiasm. A number of these organizations provided valuable feedback and updates, which helped me to ensure that the content is as accurate and current as possible.

I would also like to thank my husband for his unwavering support and encouragement.

Kids' Clubs

and

Organizations

A Comprehensive UK Guide

By Diane Mannion

Copyright Notice

R07

Contents

Introduction

Keeping children occupied is something that concerns many parents and others involved in the care of children, such as grandparents, foster parents, nannies and nursery nurses. If children become bored they can soon get up to all sorts of mischief as they look for ways of entertaining themselves and exploring the world around them. At times it can be infuriating, for example, when you find your newly decorated living room strewn with bright pink paint across the walls because your child wanted to copy daddy.

Although occasions like this can try your patience, children who behave in this way often don't realise that they are doing anything wrong. It is a natural part of their development since children have very active minds, are full of energy and are eager to learn. However, it is important to channel all this energy and enthusiasm in the right way. That's where kids' clubs can be extremely useful.

This book is packed with details regarding the various types of clubs and organizations that are available for children in the UK. Along with children's groups that you are probably already familiar with, we provide ideas on other clubs and organizations that you might not previously have considered. Because of the vast number of children's groups and organizations in the country, it would be impossible to list full details of them all in a book of this size. However, what this book does provide is ideas, information and inspiration for parents regarding the numerous valuable opportunities that are open to children of all ages. It acts as a starting point by fuelling you with ideas, then pointing to sources of further information to enable you to find groups in your locality that suit your children's interests and abilities.

The types of clubs that your children prefer could change as they get older. For instance, parent and toddler groups are aimed at pre-school children whereas the Duke of Edinburgh's Award is aimed at teenagers. Nevertheless, some children may join clubs which turn out to be a lifetime activity, for example, a dance class or drama group.

Benefits of Kids' Clubs

By involving your children in clubs and organizations you will find that not only does it keep them entertained and take the pressure off you, but they can also learn valuable skills in the process. Kids' clubs can help with physical, intellectual and social development whilst keeping children out of mischief. Being a member of a club is also a healthier and more fulfilling way of spending time than being involved in more sedentary pastimes, such as watching TV or playing computer games.

As children grow into teenagers it is even more important to engage them in worthwhile activities and give them a sense of purpose. For many teenagers this can reduce the risk of them becoming involved in drugs or crime. The various clubs and groups that are available can allow your children to learn how to work as a team, or help them to develop as an individual as they take responsibility for their own actions.

In areas where they have good skills they may have the chance to take on a leadership role; an opportunity that they may otherwise have missed out on. Voluntary work can be particularly good for teaching teenagers how their actions can impact others. This type of work can help to nurture their caring side enabling them to develop into responsible adults who value the lives of others and empathise with other people's situations.

Nurturing Talent

You may discover new talents that you didn't realise your child had, and it may give him a chance to explore new outlets for his skills. For example, your child may thrive by being involved in something creative, a caring role or a sporting venture. Most children have talents in at least one area, and if a child isn't gifted academically, his self-esteem will be boosted if he is involved in something that he is particularly good at, or something that he enjoys or finds worthwhile.

Things to Consider

There are a number of factors that you should take into account when deciding on clubs or activities for your children:

1) Make sure that the activity is appropriate for your child's age group. If you try to involve him before he is ready he will not get the full benefit from the club and may even become frustrated if he struggles with the activities. He will also be comforted by the fact that there are other children of a similar age in the group.

2) Think about your schedule and whether the opening times of the club suit you. If you are run off your feet driving your children here, there and everywhere, you may come to see it as an added pressure. It is also important not to overburden your children to the point that their activities become a chore rather than a pleasure.

3) Look into the cost of the club. Although many of the clubs and organizations featured in this book are relatively cheap, some can work out expensive. This applies in particular to those activities where there are associated costs, for example, the purchase of costumes, kits or equipment. With sports there can be additional costs if your child is entered for

medals or certificates. If it will be too expensive for you to afford, is there a cheaper alternative or a similar club that doesn't charge as much?

4) If you want your child to befriend other children at the club it may be best to choose one that is local so that they can also interact outside the group. Likewise, you could find that you build friendships with other parents through kids' clubs.

5) Look into the safety aspects of the club. Requirements will vary depending on the type of club or activity and you will probably have your own priorities when it comes to your children's health and safety, but here are some pointers to think about:

- Have the staff undertaken CRB checks?

- Are the staff qualified to work with children?

- Is the equipment well maintained?

- Is there a designated first-aider in the group?

Reputable groups should be happy to discuss these issues with you to put your mind at ease.

6) Please note that any costs and other details given in this book were accessed during the research stage. Therefore, these details could have altered slightly since that time.

Convincing a Resistant Child

If you've found a club that you feel would provide a good experience for your child, but he is reluctant to go, try to find out the reasons behind his reluctance. Approach his objections in a calm and comforting manner as you don't want matters to escalate to the point where he doesn't even want to talk about it.

Once you have found the reasons behind his reluctance you can offer some encouragement. It may be that he is nervous about being faced with a room full of strangers or frightened that he won't be very good at the activity. You can offer him words of reassurance or take positive action to enforce those words. For example, you could arrange for him to attend with a friend, or you can ask the organizers if you can sit and watch for the first couple of sessions.

It is important to take his opinion into account. If he has really strong objections or he is reluctant for a good reason then it is best not to push too hard. If he joins a club that he really dislikes it will only make him unhappy and he is unlikely to excel at something that he isn't happy with.

How this Book is Organized

To make it easy for parents and carers to access information on the various types of clubs available, we have broken this book down into chapters. Each chapter concentrates on a particular group of clubs or activities, for example, sports clubs, or parent and toddler groups. In each chapter we give some background information about the particular type of club together with details of: who can join (including age requirements), the benefits of joining the club, approximate costs, how to find out more and how parents and carers can become involved (if appropriate). As well as the general benefits outlined above, each type of club will have its own specific benefits, and we have therefore included this section in each chapter.

We haven't set out to cover every single club in the UK as there are so many of them, with lots of regional variations. Instead, we have based this book on types of clubs with each chapter giving you an insight into that particular type. Every chapter is packed full of ideas of how to access clubs in your area to cater to your child's interests. This gives you an excellent starting point.

Many parents worry about the cost of involving their children in extra-curricular activities, but many of the clubs mentioned in this book are surprisingly inexpensive to join and some are even free. Therefore, we have included a 'cost' section for each chapter to give you an idea of the prices for each of the types of clubs.

Additionally, at the end of each chapter we have given a list of valuable resources, where appropriate, to help you should you wish to pursue a particular interest for your child or become involved yourself. This could, for instance, include the contact details for any associations or bodies that regulate the particular type of club. Our sections that are headed 'Becoming Involved as a Parent' refer to all adults involved in the care of children, but we have used the word 'parent' for brevity. The last chapter of this book also covers ways in which you can find out more information.

Although 'Kids' Clubs and Organizations' has plenty of useful information about clubs and organizations that you can get your kids involved in, it is by no means an exhaustive list. You may well find other clubs and groups that we haven't covered. However, we sincerely hope that you will find this book useful and that it will inspire you to explore new ways in which to keep your children involved in worthwhile and rewarding activities.

Chapter 1 - Toy Libraries

Overview

Toy libraries began in 1967. The person responsible for their origins was Jill Norris, a Froebel trained teacher who realised how vital toys were for the development of her two children who had disabilities. She got together with other families with special needs and together they would arrange meetings in order to swap toys, exchange views and organize fundraising for the purchase of special toys. The value of toy libraries to the community was soon recognised and by 1973 the scope had widened giving all children the opportunity to borrow toys.

There are now more than 1000 toy libraries in the UK catering for about 250,000 children. These are situated in a wide range of places including schools, nurseries, libraries and community centres. They are often run by volunteers, but some are run by paid workers and others are offered as a service by professionals, such as nursery teachers, school teachers, health workers and social workers.

Toy libraries don't just loan toys; many of them offer play sessions that children can attend with their parents. Often the staff there will also give advice to parents regarding the types of toys that are suitable for their children's ages and abilities. Toy libraries provide a valuable service as children learn through play, and they allow many families in deprived areas to access expensive toys that they might otherwise not be able to afford.

Many toy libraries offer facilities for parents and carers to meet and have a chat and refreshments while the children are busy playing. Sometimes toy libraries are part of a number of facilities all based at the same centre, for example, parent and toddler groups, and playgroups. Dependent on where the toy library is located, professionals may be on hand to offer advice about parenting issues.

The National Association for Toy and Leisure Libraries (NATLL) was established in 1972. It is a national body that provides ongoing help and advice to existing toy and leisure libraries and helps new ones to set up. In June 2011 NATLL became a part of the National Children's Bureau (NCB). The Arm of the NCB that is responsible for toy libraries is now known as Play Matters in England and it continues to offer the same type of support to toy libraries as NATLL previously provided. You can find out more about this organization at: www.ncb.org.uk/play-matters. In Scotland, the organization that looks after toy libraries is the Smart Play Network at:

www.smartplaynetwork.org.

Who can join?

Membership requirements vary for each toy library. Some are for children with disabilities only; others serve mainstream children as well as children with disabilities. As a general rule, most toy libraries loan toys to mainstream children up to five years of age and children with disabilities at all ages. However, some toy libraries allow mainstream children up to eight years of age to borrow toys.

Benefits

Toy libraries offer many benefits to children and parents/carers. Amongst these are:-

- The opportunity to borrow toys at little or no cost
- A chance for children to meet and play with others
- The possibility of trying out expensive toys before making a decision to purchase them
- Advice for parents on choosing good quality toys that will help to educate and stimulate children
- An insight for parents into their children's capabilities
- Play sessions teach children how to share with others
- Children with special needs can find toys suitable for their abilities
- The ability for parents to meet others living locally

- Access to help and advice from professionals for many parents who may have problems that they are unwilling to discuss in a more formal environment
- A chance for adults to improve their parenting skills

Costs

Costs vary for different toy libraries, but they are usually very cheap, and, in some cases, free. Many toy libraries charge an initial fee for membership, then a set amount for each toy borrowed, dependent on the size of the toy.

How to Find a Toy Library

The National Children's Bureau (NCB) has a page of links on its website, which shows some details of toy libraries. You can view this at:

www.ncb.org.uk/play-matters/useful-links#toy%20library. In Scotland the Smart Play Network has details of toy libraries in Scotland. You can find out more at:

www.smartplaynetwork.org/toy-libraries/#comment-217.

Alternatively, you could try asking at the reference section of your local library or at the information department of your local government offices. Many local authorities have an A to Z of services on their websites. If you cannot find a listing under 'toy libraries' then you may find toy libraries listed under 'children's services' or 'children's centres'.

There is also an International Toy Libraries Association at:

www.itla-toylibraries.org/pages/home/, offering membership to toy libraries throughout the world as well as individuals who are involved with toy libraries.

Starting Your Own Toy Library

The NCB has a publication called 'Nuts and Bolts' which gives advice and information on setting up a toy library. It is available from the website at a cost of £10 for non-members of Play Matters or £5 for members. If you are thinking of starting your own toy library then it is worthwhile joining NCB - Play Matters as it enables you to access further sources of support and advice as well as discounts on publications. Membership of NCB costs from £70 per annum for individuals and from £100 per annum for organizations.

Volunteering

If you want to become involved with toy libraries but prefer not to run your own, then you could help out at your local toy library. Ask if they are looking for volunteers and check whether you will need any special skills or checks. The NCB are also looking for volunteers and you can find out more at: www.ncb.org.uk/support-us/volunteer-for-us.

Chapter 2 - Parent and Toddler Groups

Overview

Parent and toddler groups are for pre-school children who attend with their parents, grandparents, childminders, carers or guardians. Although the adults that attend most parent and toddler groups are predominantly mums, this is changing and more fathers are starting to attend.

These groups generally take place in community centres, churches, sports centres, schools, nurseries and other public buildings, and are run by volunteers including some of the parents and carers that attend. As the groups are usually run on a volunteer basis they appreciate input from parents and carers with tasks like helping to set up the activities or tidying the equipment away.

Occasionally you may find groups that are run by private companies, such as indoor adventure play centres or soft play centres. These private companies usually charge lower prices for parent and toddler sessions than their standard prices as this gives them custom during quiet periods. It also means that they can compete with the prices charged by volunteer groups.

Parent and toddler groups offer a range of activities, which help children to learn new skills and socialise. They can prepare children for school, especially if they follow the Foundation Stage Goals for pre-school children. Activities differ from group to group but can include:

- Play with large toys, which teaches children gross motor skills
- Group singing and storytelling, which teaches children social skills
- Crafts including painting, drawing, sticking and baking
- Small games, books and puzzles
- Role-play through dressing up
- Educational visits from people such as firemen and policemen

Some groups also have an area for babies where they can use activity toys that are age appropriate, for instance, baby gyms. Craft activities can be themed so you might receive a hand-made Christmas card from your child or an Easter treat, for example.

Parent and toddler groups usually have an allotted period when parents and carers can purchase drinks and snacks at low cost. Apart from activities for children, these groups give parents and carers a chance to chat and get to know each other.

Who can join?

Despite the name 'parent and toddler groups' they are open to anyone who attends with a pre-school child who is under their care. Most groups will allow you to attend with children from birth to the under 5s. Don't be embarrassed if your baby doesn't seem to get much out of the group as you will also benefit from attending. Additionally, the sooner your child attends a group, the sooner he will be open to the wide range of learning opportunities and activities that are available.

There is no limit to the number of parent and toddler groups that you can attend so if you and your child enjoy this outlet you could attend several a week if you want. However, some groups will have a waiting list so it is best to add your name to the list as soon as possible. Another factor is that often you don't have to live in the area where the parent and toddler group is situated so you will be able to attend other groups with friends who live in different areas. It also means that if you have a parent and toddler group that is nearby, but across the border of a neighbouring borough, you will still be able to attend the group.

Benefits

Parent and toddler groups offer many advantages, both for children and for the people who attend with them: These include:

- A chance for children to learn a wide range of pre-school skills, which can help prepare them for school

- An opportunity for toddlers to practice social skills through interaction with their peers
- A means of keeping young children entertained for part of the day so that they become less bored and restless in the home
- A way to keep children happy whilst they are involved in enjoyable activities
- A break for parents and a chance to make friends with other parents
- An opportunity for parents to seek advice and compare experiences with other parents

Costs

Costs are low and some groups charge as little as £1, which covers the costs of hiring the building, insurance and materials for arts and crafts. Some groups also use funds to purchase new equipment but much of the large equipment often comes from donations. Charges are usually per child and there is sometimes a discount if there is more than one child attending from the same family.

How to Find a Parent and Toddler Group

You can find out about parent and toddler groups in your area through the family information service search facility at:

www.daycaretrust.org.uk/findyourFIS.
Alternatively, you may find that your health visitor

or local library will keep a list of parent and toddler groups in your area. Local authorities can also be a useful source of information about groups in the area and most local authorities have their own comprehensive websites full of information about services in your region.

Additionally, many Sure Start Centres either operate a toddler group or can give you details of those in your area. You can find where your nearest Sure Start Centre is at:

http://childrenscentresfinder.direct.gov.uk/childrens centresfinder/.

Starting your Own Parent and Toddler Group

If you are thinking of starting a parent and toddler group you can get information and advice from your family information service at:

http://www.daycaretrust.org.uk/nafis. As mentioned above, this website has a search facility at:

www.daycaretrust.org.uk/findyourFIS to enable you to find your local family information service. They will advise you on such matters as:

- Finding a venue for your group
- Raising funds to set up the group
- Managing the finances
- Putting procedures in place and setting up a committee

- Checking the safety of the venue

When you set up a parent and toddler group you do not have to register with Offsted since it is the parents and carers that are responsible for the care of their children rather than the staff of the parent and toddler group. However, you will need to follow regulations relating to health and safety, fire safety and the Equality Act. Your family information service can provide advice relating to all these areas.

Another good source of information is the Pre-school Learning Alliance and their website has a section on parent and toddler groups at:

https://www.pre-school.org.uk/parents/baby-and-toddler-groups. As well as using the website as a source of information you can also become a member of the Pre-school Learning Alliance, which entitles you to a range of benefits for your parent and toddler group. These include: a legal helpline, low-cost insurance and discounted publications, for example.

If you have joined a parent and toddler group but feel that you could add value to their operation, you could get involved by helping out and sharing your ideas. By becoming a regular helper you may have the opportunity to join the committee so that you can put your suggestions across to other committee members.

Chapter 3 - Playgroups

Overview

Playgroups are usually run by voluntary organizations such as churches, and after school clubs. However, they differ from nursery schools because they are not normally open every day and the environment is less formal than with nursery schools, which are generally part of a school. Also, playgroups are likely to take children from a younger age than nurseries. The normal age for attendance at a playgroup is two and a half to three although this differs from group to group and some take children as young as two. Nursery age, on the other hand, is a minimum of three, and as nursery places are limited, it can be difficult to get your child a place in a nursery school until the year before they are due to attend school. In some cases this could mean that your child is almost four years of age.

Playgroups usually run one or two sessions a week, each of which is a couple of hours long. Although they have similar activities to parent and toddler groups, children normally attend alone rather than with their parents or carers. However, many playgroups welcome extra help so you could ask about helping out if you want to make sure that your child is fitting in well. It may not be a good idea to help out at every session as this would detract from one of the advantages of a playgroup. This advantage lies in helping your child adapt to an environment outside the home, which prepares him for school.

Playgroups generally offer the following types of activities for children:

- Arts and crafts including drawing, painting and play dough
- Board games and jigsaw puzzles
- Role-play and dressing up
- Storytelling and picture books
- Sing along time to teach them group participation and social skills
- Group games to help them with social skills
- Play with large toys (usually outdoors, but sometimes indoors if the group doesn't have outdoor facilities)

Playgroups usually have between ten and twenty children and the adults running the group should be at a ratio of one adult per eight children. In accordance with the law, 50% of those adults must be qualified play leaders or play assistants.

Partnership Playgroups (Scotland)

In Scotland the system is different and they offer Partnership Playgroups rather than playgroups. Although Partnership Playgroups are owned and managed by the community in a similar way to playgroups, they differ because they offer an education and level of care that meets the same standards as state nurseries. This means that they have to be registered with the Social Care and Social Work Improvement Scotland, and undergo regular checks and inspections to ensure that they conform to the required standards. Also, when a child turns three he is entitled to a place at a Partnership Playgroup, which is funded by the Government, in a similar way to nursery school in England. However, because they are run by the community there is a higher level of parental involvement than at nursery school.

Who can join?

Playgroups are for pre-school aged children. The age when your child will be ready for playgroup will depend on the guidelines of each individual group. It will normally be from two and a half or three years of age, but a few groups accept children from the age of two. It is important to note that many playgroups have long waiting lists so it is essential to put your child's name on the waiting list as soon as possible.

Most groups will also specify that your child must be out of nappies and 'dry' before he can attend a group. It is normal for children to have the occasional 'accident' especially when they are introduced to a new environment, and most playgroups are understanding regarding this. However, playgroups do not have sufficient staff to deal with the regular changing of nappies and clothes so you should ensure that you don't send your child until he is dry.

Although you may find your child has a few 'accidents' when he first attends the group, this will settle down with time, and you will probably find that he improves because he will want to be like the other children. Additionally, most groups have 'toilet time' when they encourage children to visit the toilet and wash their hands afterwards.

Benefits

Playgroups offer many benefits for pre-school children including:

- Promoting independence and getting children ready for school by teaching them what is expected of them and how to follow rules
- Preparing children for school by easing them out of the home and into a new environment
- Providing a transitional stage between home and school so that your child is not overwhelmed by the sheer size of school and the many older children

- Improvements in social skills through mixing with other children in the same age group
- A chance for children to express themselves through role play
- Learning opportunities through puzzles, books, and arts and crafts
- Opportunities to improve gross motor skills through play with large toys

Apart from the benefits to children, playgroups also give mums a break or a chance to catch up on chores.

Costs

An advantage of playgroups is that they are normally low in cost, unlike day nurseries, which are privately run and charge high fees. You can expect to pay as little as £2 a session for a playgroup although this varies so it is best to check beforehand. Some groups also ask parents or carers to contribute materials for the activities that take place in the playgroup.

How to Find a Playgroup

You can find details of Playgroups in your area through a Sure Start Centre. Many of these offer childcare but you usually have to pay unless your child has reached the age of three or four and qualifies for free State education. They also offer many free services, such as the provision of health visitors and midwives, and some run parent and toddler groups. You can find your nearest Sure Start Centre by using the link:

http://childrenscentresfinder.direct.gov.uk/childrens centresfinder/.

Other ways to find out about Playgroups in your area are through your local library, clinic, health visitor or local government website.

Chapter 4 - Playbuses

Overview

Playbuses date back to 1969 in the UK when a Liverpool GP came up with the idea of converting a bus into a play area for children. The idea was soon taken up in other cities and by 1973 the National Playbus Association was formed to cater to the needs of the many playbuses operating in the UK. Initially the association was run by volunteers, but in 1978 the Department of Health agreed to provide funding for playbuses, which were then aimed at children under five.

Since that time the level of funding has fluctuated, but the use of converted buses and other vehicles to provide community services has grown steadily. Mobile vehicles have the advantage of being able to provide community services in remote areas or areas where there are insufficient numbers of community buildings. Vehicles other than buses that have been converted include coaches, trucks, trailers, and vans.

Some playbuses offer a number of different services at various times. The number of services provided by playbuses has also expanded and although they still cater to children under the age of eight, more than 50% provide other types of services. In fact, the National Playbus Association changed its name in 2010 and is now known as 'Working on Wheels'. This organization supports various types of mobile community projects in the UK such as:

- Parent and toddler groups, and crèches

- Youth centres

- Toy libraries

- IT centres and education centres

- Information centres

- Health advice centres

- Holiday play centres

- Centres for the disabled

Working on Wheels offers support and advice for groups operating playbuses and mobile units, and now has more than 200 members. It also provides training and cheaper insurance.

Who can join?

Whether you can access the services provided by a playbus or mobile unit will be subject to a number of factors. These factors include: whether there is a playbus that covers your area, the type of services that it provides and the stipulations applied by the people who run the playbus. It is best to enquire with the particular mobile unit. To find out if there is a mobile unit in your area, please refer to our section headed 'How to Find a Playbus'.

Benefits

The benefits will depend on the services offered by a particular mobile unit, but as a whole these can include:

- A chance to deliver essential services to remote or isolated areas
- Enrichment and a range of valuable activities delivered from one vehicle
- They can become a valuable hub of any community, and enable the community to share in the advantages offered
- Opportunities for community members to interact, socialise and share ideas
- Low operating overheads in comparison with permanent structures
- More flexibility than permanent structures in terms of location and versatility
- The promotion of social interaction amongst different groups in the community, bringing the community together as a whole
- The provision of a venue for planned events or community projects

As well as these general advantages, each type of service has its own benefits. For example, a mums and toddlers group that takes place in a mobile unit will offer similar benefits to those outlined in chapter 2 of this book.

Costs

Because mobile units are community based and are financed either as charities or by government grants, their charges for services are very low. For some services there is no cost. However, each individual unit will set its own prices so it is best to check with them.

How to Find a Playbus

The Working on Wheels organization has a website at: www.workingonwheels.org. At the bottom of the home page is a link called 'Useful Links'. If you select this link, this page of the website gives a full listing of Working on Wheels members throughout the UK. These are broken down into regions, such as Scotland, North West England, Midlands etc. Under each region you can find a list of towns or cities that have a mobile unit together with details of the website for each one.

Starting your own Playbus

There is a lot involved in setting up your own playbus or mobile unit, and although overall costs can be high, they compare favourably with the costs for permanent structures. You will need to balance the potential costs and the work involved against the benefits that you and your community will derive from the mobile unit. The Working on Wheels organization at:

www.workingonwheels.org provides a lot of information on the process of setting up a mobile unit. We recommend that you read this information as it will give you a good idea of what to expect.

You can access information from the publications section of the website. Working on Wheels also provides a lot of help and advice to members so it is worthwhile joining; you can find out more about membership on the website.

Chapter 5 - Dance, Theatre and Music Groups

Overview

Dance, drama and music enable children of all ages to explore their talents outside of the classroom environment. This can be particularly enriching for children who struggle academically as the focus here is not on academic achievement. For children who take pleasure in these activities the emphasis is on enjoyment, but whilst they are enjoying themselves they are learning some valuable skills. We have looked at the many benefits of these activities under our 'benefits' section in this chapter. These include, for example, confidence building and social skills.

Under the general banner of 'dance, theatre and music' there are many different options and your children may have their own preferred style. For instance, music can range from taking part in DJ sessions, or music production, to joining the local brass band. The Boys' Brigade usually has a brass band so this can provide opportunities; we have covered the Boys' Brigade in chapter 6. Another option is for your child to learn to play an instrument through private music lessons.

Dance can be traditional, such as ballet, tap or Morris Dancing; on the other hand, it can be more contemporary, such as break dancing. Drama also offers various possibilities; these can range from learning the art of role play to joining the local theatre, which may involve song and dance as well as acting. It all depends on where your child's interests lie, but don't be afraid to explore the different options. You may even find that your child has a previously undiscovered talent.

Who can join?

Dance classes are open to various age groups. However, they are likely to be banded in terms of age as children will have different physical skills according to how old they are. Some dance companies may only cater to a certain age group; others will have several classes for different age bands. If your child outgrows a dance class and there isn't another class available with that company, you should approach an alternative company and find out if they give classes for your child's age group.

Theatre classes again will be for various age groups and it all depends on the company or organization that is offering the classes. It is best to make enquiries when you find an organization that offers drama for children. We have given some suggestions on finding classes or groups in our later section headed 'How to Find a Dance, Theatre or Music Group.'

With music tuition, the age at which children can join a class or group will be specified by the group or organization that is offering the tuition. Some may stipulate that children won't be ready to learn a musical instrument before a certain age. Another barrier could be cost as private lessons can be expensive. However, there are cheaper options you can explore and these are covered in subsequent sections of this chapter.

Benefits

The benefits will be subject to the type of performing arts your child becomes involved with; whether this will be dance, theatre or music. In some cases children become involved in more than one of these, and sometimes all three, since they can overlap. In a musical production, for example, there are likely to be actors, dancers and musicians taking part as well as children that have more than one of these skills.

Dance, theatre and music will share some of the same benefits, but they will also have their own individual benefits. We have therefore divided this section into three sub-sections, which are: Benefits of Dance, Benefits of Theatre and Benefits of Music. Where these activities share the same benefits, those benefits will be listed under more than one section.

Benefits of Dance

- The physical aspect helps children to be more healthy
- It improves strength, flexibility, balance, co-ordination, agility, posture and focus
- Dance is a good stress reliever and helps children to feel more relaxed
- Children learn to interact with others through dancing as a group
- It teaches children self-discipline
- It can help to improve confidence and self-esteem
- Dance fosters creativity and self-expression

Benefits of Theatre

- It gives children a chance to communicate orally and practice public speaking
- It helps to improve confidence and self-esteem
- The ability to communicate orally can improve social skills
- Children can also practice, and learn to interpret, non-verbal forms of communication, such as body language
- Drama helps children become more creative and teaches them self-expression
- It helps to broaden a child's imagination, which is important for developing original thoughts and ideas

- The learning of lines can help to improve memory
- It helps to relieve stress and enables students to feel more relaxed
- Drama helps with literacy skills

Benefits of Music

- It helps children with language skills
- The teaching of rhythm can help children to learn maths
- Learning music helps children to develop their concentration
- Musical performance can improve confidence and raise self-esteem
- Communication through music can help with social skills
- Taking part in music helps children to become more relaxed and less stressed
- It enables self expression and creativity
- It helps with hand-eye co-ordination and motor skills
- Children learn to be more patient and to persevere when learning an instrument

Costs

Costs can vary tremendously according to who is providing the service. At the lower end of the cost scale are charities that run groups for children in deprived areas. These vary from area to area and can range across the whole spectrum of the performing arts. This gives children an outlet for their creativity and brings them off the streets by involving them in worthwhile activities. Because these are provided by charities they are most likely to be free or at very low cost.

At the higher end of the scale are private one to one lessons usually for music tuition. If one to one tuition proves too expensive you could try group tuition instead. However, for group music tuition, your child would have to be of a similar standard to the rest of the group. Therefore, if music lessons are something that you really feel your child will gain from, you could try investing in private tuition until he has reached a sufficient standard to partake in a group.

Apart from the above two alternatives there are a range of other options at different prices. A point to note is that, generally, private lessons will be more expensive than those that are charity funded or provided by local authorities. However, some private tutors come into schools to offer dance, drama or music, and often charge at a lower rate to schools than they would do for private lessons.

In the following section we give some ideas for finding various groups for performing arts. It is worthwhile exploring the options and enquiring about charges. However, an important consideration, apart from monthly or weekly charges or upfront course fees, is the associated costs. These can include, for example, drama and dance costumes, dancing shoes, purchase of musical instruments, costs of awards, medals and certificates etc.

Many dance companies will charge a relatively low amount for children's dance and drama classes, but the associated costs soon add up. For instance, if your child was to attend ballet and tap dancing classes with a private company you would likely need to buy a ballet dress, ballet shoes and tap dancing shoes. You would then also need to pay for any medals, awards or certificates that they had won and for costumes for any production that your child might appear in.

It is possible to get some help with associated costs. For example, with local authority music tuition schemes or music tuition provided through schools, instruments may be available on loan. If you have concerns about the overall cost of music tuition, drama instruction or dance classes, it is important to find out as many details as possible relating to cost before committing.

How to Find a Dance, Theatre or Music Group

The availability of groups is likely to depend very much on where you live, but classes and tuition are run by a combination of the private and public sector so there should be opportunities in most areas. Here are some avenues to try:

- A good place to start is your local authority as it may have a scheme for music, drama or dance tuition for children, and should give you an idea of the age groups that classes apply to, venues, times and prices. You can find a list of all local authorities in the UK at: www.direct.gov.uk/en/Dl1/Directories/Local councils/AToZOfLocalCouncils/index.htm. If your local authority doesn't have its own scheme, it should be able to give you details of classes or groups in your area including those that are run by charities.

- Your local library is another good source of information, and will usually have a list of classes in your area.

- Try entering the search terms 'children's dance classes + (your town/city)', 'children's drama classes + (your town/city)', or 'children's music classes + (your town/city)' in an Internet search engine or look up 'dance', 'music', or 'drama' in your local telephone directory.

- If your child's school has private tutors offering after school classes they will usually notify you by letter so make sure that your child lets you have any letters that are sent by school. If your child's school has offered classes in the past you could ask about plans for the coming academic year.

- Other schools may offer classes to pupils who don't attend that school, especially art academies, which have readily accessible facilities and often have a rich timetable of events.
- Dance schools which offer dance classes for adults, will also often provide children's dance classes.
- If you find a private music tutor, ask him/her what the charges are for individual and group tuition and whether you can get a discount for payment up front, or whether there are any other special payment arrangements or discounts.
- Colleges with facilities for the performing arts also sometimes offer children's classes.
- Many Boys' and Girls' Brigades have a brass band that children can join.
- Local theatres also sometimes offer drama, dance and music classes for children, and the children often get opportunities to take part in amateur theatre productions.
- Private dance teachers may offer classes at church halls or community centres for children of varying age groups.

Becoming Involved as a Parent

Many dance, music and theatre groups welcome adult helpers. Nevertheless, in some instances you may have to have specialist qualifications or experience. It is therefore worthwhile enquiring with your group of choice to find out whether they have any particular requirements.

Chapter 6 - The Boys' Brigade and the Girls' Brigade

Overview

The Boys' and Girls' Brigade are separate organizations to those of the Boy Scouts and Girl Guides, which are covered in chapter 7. They are also distinct from each other, so we will start by giving an overview of each.

Boys' Brigade

Sir William Alexander Smith started the Boys' Brigade in Glasgow, Scotland back in 1883. It has now become a worldwide organization, which has a Christian basis and provides activities for boys from the ages of 5 to 18. The Boys' Brigade has a million members worldwide and more than 65,000 in the UK. It is divided into the regions of England, Scotland, Wales, Ireland and Northern Ireland, and there are regional centres where training courses take place as well as many other events. Each region (except Scotland) has a number of Districts; these Districts are made up of Battalions, which in turn are made up of Companies. There are 1500 Companies throughout the UK.

Each Company usually runs in partnership with a church and carries out most of its activities on the church premises. This fits in with the aspect of the Boy's Brigade's objectives which relates to the provision of Christian teaching. Apart from pastimes that take place in church, there are also many opportunities for outdoor pursuits. Some of the wide spectrum of interests offered by the Boys' Brigade include:

- Games and physical challenges
- Arts, crafts, cookery and hobbies such as collecting
- Music and drama
- Puzzles, quizzes and mental games
- Treasure hunts
- Prayer, worship and Christian teaching
- Conservation and involvement with the local community
- Theme nights

Within every Company is a number of sections based on age and these are detailed under our section 'Who can join?' From the age of 11 boys are awarded according to their achievements through programmes. Each programme covers a number of areas where boys earn points for taking part plus a number of compulsory areas. Once boys attain a certain number of points and fulfil the compulsory areas of the programme they are given an award (or badge). These programmes give boys the opportunity to learn about health and lifestyle, get involved in the community, go on camping trips, learn about nature and the environment, play sports and games, and take part in many other interesting and worthwhile activities and events.

Some of the badges are gained through achievements in the Duke of Edinburgh's programme. You will find details of the Duke of Edinburgh's Award in chapter 17 of this book.

Girls' Brigade

The Girls' Brigade was formed as a result of the amalgamation of three different bodies in 1965, which were: The Girls' Life Brigade (established in England in 1902), The Girls' Brigade (Ireland) (established in Dublin in 1893) and The Girls' Guildry (established in Scotland in 1900). The following notes relate to the Girls' Brigade in England and Wales. In Scotland and Northern Ireland the Girls Brigade operates slightly differently, for example, the names of programmes will not be the same.

In a similar way to the Boys' Brigade, the Girls' Brigade is a Christian based group, which offers enrichment through religious teaching combined with activities aimed at girls of various ages.

The Girls' Brigade is a worldwide organization and it is divided into 5 areas known as fellowships. These are: Europe, Asia, Africa, the Caribbean and the Americas, and the Pacific. Each local group is known as a Company and there are more than 3000 of these worldwide with more than 126,000 members.

Girls from the ages of 4 to 18 can join the Girls' Brigade and it is divided into age ranges in a similar way to the Boy's Brigade. We give details of the different age bands in the next section. The activities offered depend on the age range and on the individual group, but generally they can include:

- Arts and crafts
- Baking
- Games
- Involvement with the local community
- Drama and dance
- Health education
- Learning about the planet, and other countries and cultures
- Religious education
- Personal development
- Weekend trips, activities and events
- Fund raising and charity donations

During weekly meetings children explore a number of topics that usually last for five weeks. On completion of each topic children receive awards in the form of a certificate or badge. Younger children keep a sticker book and they receive a sticker when they complete a topic. The older children have a journal which they use to record their experiences as a member of the Girls' Brigade.

Most of the Girls' Brigade groups also enable children to take part in further award schemes including: The Duke of Edinburgh's Award, The Queen's Award and Young Leaders' Training. You can find out more about The Duke of Edinburgh's Award in chapter 17 of this book, and your local Company will be able to give you details of the other award schemes.

Who can join?

All children are eligible to join either the Boys' Brigade or the Girls' Brigade depending on their gender and regardless of their faith or background, although Christian teachings form a large part of the activities of these organizations. Each Company is broken down into sections according to ages, as follows:

Age Ranges for Boys

- Anchor Boys - Age 5 to 8
- Junior Section - Age 8 to 11
- Company Section - Age 11 to 15
- Seniors - Age 15 to 18

Each of the sections has its own programme of activities and events and children within these sections work towards awards based on their achievements. Activities are broken down into various areas so that children receive mental, physical, creative and spiritual stimulation as well as getting involved in the local community. Companies also have theme nights which the different sections may take part in together.

Age Ranges for Girls

- n:vestigate (for Explorers) - Age 4 to 8
- n:gage (for Juniors) - Age 7 to 11
- n:counta (for Seniors) - Age 10 to 14
- n:spire (for Brigaders) - Age 13 to 18

There is a slight overlap in ages as some girls will be ready to progress to the next section sooner than others. Each section has a theme of activities and events which are appropriate for that age range. These are: for n:vestigate - fun and friendship, for n:gage - excitement and challenges, for n:counta - new experiences and lots of laughs and for n:spire - new opportunities and a space to be you.

Benefits

Both the Boys' and Girls' Brigade provide a range of benefits, including:

- Teaching children a variety of useful skills
- Providing opportunities to take a leadership role
- Encouraging decision making and taking responsibility
- Educating children about the needs of others and promoting a caring approach through projects that can help those in need

- Providing Christian teaching for children
- Opportunities to gain social skills and an appreciation of the needs and aspirations of others
- Giving children a sense of achievement when they receive their awards

Costs

You will usually be asked to make a weekly contribution, which is generally very low and helps to cover materials etc. Typical charges are between £1 and £1.50 per week but this differs from Company to Company. Funds can be collected weekly, monthly or per term depending on the individual group. It will also be necessary to purchase a uniform for your child. Some Companies have a scheme where members bring in their old uniforms so that they can be resold at a reduced price to new members. Companies that have a band will normally let members borrow instruments.

How to Find a Boys' or Girls' Brigade Company

Firstly, try the churches in your local area to find out whether they run a Boys' or Girls' Brigade. If you don't manage to find one you could try contacting the Boys' or Girls' Brigade through their websites. The Boys' Brigade website has an online feedback form for comments and enquiries and the

Girls' Brigade website has a contact page. The website addresses are:

Boys' Brigade -

www.boys-brigade.org.uk/index.htm;

Girls' Brigade - www.girlsb.org.uk/.

Becoming an Adult Volunteer with the Boys' or Girls' Brigade

Both the Boys' Brigade and the Girls' Brigade have a page on their website detailing how you as a parent can get involved as a volunteer. The website links are - for the Boys' Brigade: www.boys-brigade.org.uk/volunteering.htm, and for the Girls' Brigade: www.girlsb.org.uk/be-part-of-it-_32/. You could also approach your local Company to offer your services as a volunteer helper.

Chapter 7 - Scouts and Guides

Overview

The Scout Association and Girlguiding UK are completely separate organizations from the Boys' and Girls' Brigade which we covered in chapter 6.

The Scout Association

The Scout Association offers activities and development opportunities to 400,000 girls and boys in the UK from the ages of 6 to 25. It is part of a worldwide organization with more than 28 million members in 216 countries. Its focus is on personal development which is achieved through a number of areas; these are physical, social, intellectual and spiritual. The Association offers adventure and activities that are designed to encourage young people to be self reliant, caring, responsible and committed. This means that they will be involved in teamwork, outdoor exploration and the community, as well as taking part in new activities and experiences.

Scouting was founded by Lord Baden-Powell in 1907. He was a former soldier who was interested in how boys used their initiative under pressure. Because of his interests he set up a camp for 20 boys from various backgrounds to study his ideas. The movement was established as a result of that first camp.

In terms of structure, The Scout Association is divided into counties in England and Northern Ireland and areas in Scotland and Wales. There are 114 Scout Counties and each of these has a number of networks. The Scout Counties are sub-divided into over 1000 Scout Districts. In turn, each of these Scout Districts has an Explorer Scout Unit for Scouts between the ages of 14 and 18 and a number of Scout Groups.

There are nearly 10,000 Scout Groups in the UK altogether and most of these consist of a Beaver Scout Colony, a Cub Scout Pack and a Scout Troop. The different types of Scouts, such as Beavers, Cubs etc are for set ages and these are detailed in our section headed 'Who can join?'

The Scout Association has a set programme of training, activities and awards covering all age groups. For the older groups the emphasis is very much on action and adventure. Some typical activities (dependant on age groups) are:

- Learning about health and personal safety,
- Learning about science, nature and technology
- Developing a caring nature by finding out about the needs of others in the community
- Camping, hiking, rock climbing, map reading and pioneering
- Sailing and canoeing

- Abseiling, gliding and parascending
- First Aid
- Electronics
- Motor mechanics
- Photography
- Amateur radio

The Scout Association gives regular awards and badges based on achievements. Badges can relate to attainment of particular skills or taking part in specific pursuits; so for example, there are badges for camping, badges for healthy eating and badges for IT. Challenge awards are aligned to The Scout Association's balanced programme and are generally more difficult to attain than badges. There are also a number of higher level awards available, such as Bronze, Silver, Gold, Platinum and Diamond Chief Scout's Awards as well as awards for attendance. Additionally, older members can take part in the Duke of Edinburgh's Award; this is covered in chapter 17 of this book.

Girl Guides

The Guiding Association in the UK operates under the name of Girlguiding UK. It is part of the organization known as the World Association of Girl Guides and Girl Scouts (WAGGGS), which operates in 145 countries and is the world's biggest women's organization with more than 10 million members worldwide.

Girlguiding UK has about half a million members and is the biggest voluntary organization for girls and women in the UK. It is split into 28,000 units (or groups) and there are more than 80,000 leaders and helpers. Girlguiding UK is open to girls and young women aged from 5 to 25 (or from age 4 in Northern Ireland). It teaches them a range of skills and presents them with many opportunities. These include a chance to make new friends, involvement in decision making situations, learning how to take care of the Environment, taking part in new experiences and adventures, and learning about the world and different cultures.

The Girl Guides Association was established in 1910 following on from the earlier formation of the Scouting Association. Girls came to the attention of Lord Baden-Powell when they gate-crashed the first Boy Scout's rally and demanded that Lord Baden-Powell should also offer something for them. As a result, the Girl Guides Association was formed under the presidency of Lord Baden-Powell's sister, Agnes Baden-Powell.

Girlguiding UK is open to all girls regardless of their circumstances or background and each of the 28,000 Guides units is subdivided into Rainbows, Brownies, Guides, and Seniors according to age. Details of the age bands are given in the following section headed, 'Who can join?'

Activities vary according to the age range but can include:

- Games and activities
- Story reading
- Computer games and their own dedicated area of the Girlguiding website
- Camping holidays and sleepovers
- Special events
- Day trips and holidays (including trips to the Girl Guides' Activity Centres)
- Arts, crafts and cookery
- Community action projects
- Sports
- Performing arts

From the ages of 7 to 10 girls can gain special interest badges for becoming involved in particular hobbies or activities, for example, circus skills or being a science investigator. As well as these badges, Girl Guides (aged 10-14) can also gain Challenge badges for good attendance.

From the ages of 14 to 25 the Senior members are encouraged to try out a variety of new experiences, such as: learning a new language, running a marathon, camping out, learning to play a musical instrument, or volunteering overseas. The type of experience and the degree of involvement is up to the individual.

Senior members can also earn a wider range of awards and qualifications, for instance, the Leadership qualification, which teaches them to run the younger members' sections. They can also take part in the Duke of Edinburgh's Award or in the many international events and projects that are open to Seniors.

Who can join?

Although traditionally the Scouts Association has been aimed at boys and the Guides aimed at girls, there is nothing to stop girls joining the Scouts and there are actually 60,000 members who are female. Any young person between the ages of 6 and 25 can become a Scout regardless of their faith or background. Unlike the Boy's Brigade it is not a Christian based organization, but is multi-faith. Girlguiding UK is also open to people of all faiths, but it is not open to boys. The Scouts and the Girl Guides are split into different sections according to age, as follows:

Age Ranges for Scouts
- Beaver Scouts - Age 6 to 8
- Cub Scouts - Age 8 to 10 and a half
- Scouts - Age 10 and a half to 14
- Explorer Scouts - Age 14 to 18
- Network - Age 18 to 25

Age Ranges for Guides

- Rainbows - Age 5 to 7 (4 to 7 in Northern Ireland)
- Brownies - Age 7 to 10
- Guides - Age 10 to 14
- Seniors - Age 14 to 25

NB Adults from the ages of 18 to 65 can be volunteers and they don't have to be members of the Guides Association to do so.

Benefits

Children can derive many benefits from joining the Scouting Association or the Girl Guides. Some of these include:

- Gaining a sense of responsibility, being encouraged to think for themselves and make decisions
- Increased social skills and confidence building
- A chance to experience new activities
- An opportunity to experience the thrill of action and adventure
- Being taught discipline
- Being taught essential life skills such as cookery
- Learning teamwork and leadership skills
- Developing an appreciation of different cultures

Costs

The costs for Scouting depend on the group but they are relatively inexpensive at between £50 and £100 per year. If fees are collected on a weekly basis this equates to only a pound or two a week, but some groups prefer to collect fees monthly, each term or annually. As well as regular fees, which help to pay for materials and the meeting venue, you will have to pay separately for any trips. All sections of the Scouts wear a uniform, which has to be purchased separately. Your Scout Group will put you in touch with specialist suppliers or you can purchase the uniform from the Scout shop at:

www.scoutshops.com/.

The Scout Association emphasises that cost should not be a barrier to membership so if you are having difficulty meeting the costs you should talk to your child's Scout Leader in confidence.

For Girlguiding UK a small annual membership fee is charged, which pays for insurance and entitles members to special discounted rates for merchandise. Girls also have to pay a small regular fee to their unit or group to cover the costs of room hire, materials etc. This varies from group to group but the cost is usually low. Girls also have to wear a uniform but most items cost less than £10 each.

How to Find a Scouts or Guides Group

To find out about Scout Groups in your area, contact the Scout Information Centre on telephone number: 0845 300 1818. Some groups have a waiting list since there are more children wanting to join the Scouts than there are adult helpers. You can find out how to be a volunteer helper in the following section and can find more information on the website at: https://members.scouts.org.uk/.

Girl Guide Units or groups are usually located in community centres or youth centres. To find a Girl Guides group in your area, contact Girlguiding UK on telephone number: 0800 1 69 59 01 or email: joinus@girlguiding.org.uk. You can also find out more information from the website at:

www.girlguiding.org.uk.

Becoming an Adult Volunteer with the Scouts or Guides

The Scout Association is in need of volunteer helpers. You can get involved as a parent helper either by contacting your local Scout Group or by filling in the Scout Organization's online form at: http://87.127.227.205/join/join_volunteer.php.

Girlguiding UK is also in need of volunteer helpers as they have 45,000 girls waiting for places. To facilitate places for another 45,000 girls, the Girl Guide Association needs a further 7,000 volunteers.

You don't have to be a member to volunteer and can find out more at:

www.girlguiding.org.uk/parents__carers/volunteer_with_girlguiding_uk.aspx.

Chapter 8 - Volunteering

Overview

There are many volunteering opportunities available for children, and these will enable them to become involved in something worthwhile. Through volunteering children can also pick up lots of valuable skills while providing much needed help to individuals and organizations. Although there are more opportunities open to the over 16s, there are still many ways in which younger children can get involved in volunteering. Here are some ideas for organizations that take volunteers, or ways in which children can get involved in volunteering:

St John Ambulance - This is open to children from the age of 5 upwards and is covered in chapter 9.

The British Red Cross - Volunteering is open to older children from age 15 upwards and is covered in chapter 10.

The Duke of Edinburgh's Award - This is open to teenagers and young people from the ages of 14 to 24 and involves volunteering as an integral part of the activities that go towards gaining the award. You will find more details in chapter 17.

Boys' and Girls' Brigade, Boy Scouts and Girl Guides - These give older members opportunities to become involved in community projects, volunteer abroad or help with the younger members' sections. These are covered in chapters 6 and 7.

Become an Online Volunteer - There are so many things that children of various ages can do online to serve a good cause. These cover a wide range of interests including computers and Internet, crafts, animal welfare, science and research, human welfare, sports and education, and many others. Activities are as diverse as playing a free online game that donates to charity, or packaging up some used books to send to Ugandan orphans who want to learn the English language. You can find out more about becoming an online volunteer in our section headed 'How to Find Volunteering Opportunities'

Your Local Volunteer Centre - There are many of these throughout the country and they will let you have details of the opportunities available in your area. We give details on locating a Volunteer Centre in our section headed 'How to Find Volunteering Opportunities'.

Through your Child's School - Many schools get involved in fundraising projects, such as sponsored silences. Nationally, hundreds of schools work in conjunction with the Giving Nation project and you can find out more in our section, 'How to Find Volunteering Opportunities'.

Who can join?

67

Anybody can volunteer, but the over 16s will probably have more opportunities open to them than under 16s. This is usually because of issues regarding safety or insurance policies. Also, for over 16s who want to volunteer in certain local authority sectors, such as at hospitals, they will have to undergo a CRB check. It can take up to six weeks for a CRB check so it is worth bearing this in mind.

If you want to find out whether specific volunteering opportunities are open to your child's age group we advise you to look at the volunteering ideas described in the chapter 'Overview' as well as any further information that we have suggested relating to these ideas.

<u>Benefits</u>

As there are such a wide range of volunteer opportunities, the benefits derived from doing volunteer work are also wide in scope. However, some of the general benefits are:

- It encourages children to adopt a caring attitude together with a wider appreciation of the needs of others
- It gives children a sense of responsibility
- Children can gain a broad range of skills related to the work that they are involved in
- Children gain confidence through interacting with others outside their usual social circle

- Some volunteer opportunities enable children to work as part of a team
- Through their involvement children learn more about the world around them
- Many people and organizations benefit from child volunteers who offer their services
- Children get a lot of pleasure and enjoyment from many of the activities

Costs

Because your child is working as a volunteer there is no cost to you for the most part. However, there may be overheads related to certain volunteer activities. For example, there may be travel expenses to certain locations where volunteer activities take place or postage costs with such activities as sending packages to people in deprived countries.

How to Find Volunteering Opportunities

The UK charity YouthNet runs the national volunteering database called 'Do it', which has a website page specifically for the under 16s. You can find it at:

www.do-it.org.uk/wanttovolunteer/aboutvolunteering/volunteeringforunder16s. This page is full of suggestions regarding volunteering opportunities for this age group.

YouthNet also works in partnership with Volunteer Centres from around the country, and many voluntary organizations, which forward details of volunteer opportunities to 'Do it'. These are then advertised on the 'Do it' website. You can find your nearest Volunteer Centre at:

www.do-it.org.uk/wanttovolunteer/aboutvolunteering/vcfinder.

For details of the wide range of online volunteering opportunities open to children, please refer to: http://helpfromhome.org/. This page gives a host of ideas for online volunteering with links to further information, which explains: how to get involved, what impact the volunteer activity will make, how much time is required and whether it will cost anything.

For information about volunteer activities involving schools, please refer to: www.g-nation.org.uk/. Giving Nation is a project of the Citizenship Foundation (www.citizenshipfoundation.org.uk) aimed at Secondary Schools and alternative educational settings. Its purpose is to encourage Secondary School children to support charities and good causes by giving their time and energy whilst developing a range of valuable skills relating to volunteering. The Giving Nation project is delivered through the curriculum so it is focused on key skills. Some of the larger national charities work hand in hand with schools to find ways of fundraising through their joint co-operation.

Some Local Authorities also run volunteer schemes, for example, Stockport Action for Voluntary Youth (SAVY at: www.stockportsavy.org.uk) helps young people in Stockport from the ages of 14 to 25 to find volunteer opportunities.

Creating your own Volunteer Opportunities

If you have children of Secondary School age you could try getting their school involved in fundraising, social enterprise, campaigning or volunteering by telling them about the Giving Nation project at: www.g-nation.org.uk/.

Other ways in which you can create volunteering opportunities for your children, or they can create opportunities themselves, are by approaching organizations directly. For example, you could try enquiring at old people's homes or pet rescue centres to find out if they need any help. For younger children in particular it is important that you accompany them to any places they approach until you feel confident that your child will be working in a safe and secure environment. Alternatively, you may find opportunities (from some of the above-mentioned sources) that you and your children could become involved in together.

Chapter 9 - St John Ambulance

Overview

The aim of St John Ambulance is to provide first aid training and knowledge to as many people as possible as this valuable training could mean, 'the difference between a life lost and a life saved'. The organization provides training in the workplace, in schools and in the community, but also provides first aid directly via its own volunteers. St John Ambulance volunteers provide additional support to ambulance services and provide first aid at public events. Additionally, they work in partnership with NHS Ambulance Service Trusts to provide a response to emergency calls until the ambulance service arrives. The volunteers that provide this service are called 'Community First Responders' and are specially trained.

St John Ambulance has a rich history, which dates back to the 11th Century with the Order of Saint John, when a hospice was set up in Jerusalem by a group of Benedictine monks to care for sick pilgrims. In 1877 the St John Ambulance Association was formed with the purpose of teaching first aid to the civilian population. Ten years later the St John Ambulance Brigade was established to deliver first aid and ambulance services by uniformed members at public events.

The organization is now known as St John Ambulance.

As well as being the leading organization for first aid training and provision in the UK, St John Ambulance has a large youth movement. It has more than 23,000 adult members and almost 20,000 young members. It also has more than 1000 ambulance and support vehicles, and its own museum and library. Furthermore, the organization now operates in many other countries throughout the world.

St John Ambulance offers a range of activities and awards to children depending on their age group. For details of the age bands for each youth group, please refer to the following section entitled, 'Who can join?' The emphasis of each youth group is on first aid, but children can take part in other activities, as follows:

Badgers

Badgers follow a varied programme of fun activities and can choose from fifteen different topics. Topics are aimed at developing the child and, as well as first aid, they include looking after the environment, personal safety, arts and crafts, and physical pursuits. Whilst taking part in these activities Badgers are working towards their Super Badger Award, which is attained in four stages. The stages are: membership paw, bronze paw, silver paw and gold paw. Badgers have to complete three topics for each of the bronze, silver and gold paw stages.

Apart from being taught first aid as part of the work towards their award, Badgers can build on this through further first aid training. Badgers attend a weekly meeting for about one and a half hours and some public events. In addition, they have the opportunity to take part in organized outdoor activities, such as camping.

Cadets

For Cadets there is a more extensive programme of activities than for Badgers with a choice of more than 100 topics. Topics cover first aid and a wide range of activities including sports, fire prevention and photography. Cadets are also taught first aid skills through various training courses depending on the age of the Cadet. They then get to use these skills at public events, and have opportunities to teach first aid to others.

The programme of activities is geared towards attainment of the Grand Prior Award. This is broken down into stages, which are: the Membership Award, Bronze Award, Silver Award, Gold Award and Grand Prior Award. The Membership Award prepares the child or young person for joining the Cadet Unit by teaching them the basics of becoming a Cadet. Former Badgers will have already received this introduction through their Follow-Me Badger

Award. For each of the Bronze and Silver Awards, Cadets have to complete eight topics, and for each of the Gold Award and the Grand Prior Award they have to complete four. With the Grand Prior Award the topics are at three different levels so that Cadets can work at a level suitable for them.

New members attend an enrolment ceremony in which they swear to follow 'The Cadet Code of Chivalry'. This code consists of a number of mottoes, which originate from the Order of St John and embrace the meaning of being a St John Cadet.

LINKS

LINKS is for young people in further education and 90% of LINKS members join when they start university, as LINKS units are affiliated with students' unions. Students can gain first aid training through joining a LINKS unit and will attend weekly meetings during term-time. Once trained, they will provide first aid within the university as well as in the local community. More experienced members can also become involved in teaching first aid skills to new members.

On top of providing valuable first aid training, LINKS units offer a variety of events to students including team building weekends and annual balls. This can help students settle into the social aspect of going away to university more easily as it gives them the opportunity to meet new people.

LINKS units are run by students so individuals may get opportunities to help manage a unit once they gain experience. Voluntary work does not only involve the provision of first aid; it also includes working with young people.

Who can join?

St John Ambulance is open to members from the age of five upwards. For children it is divided into sections depending on age as follows:

- Badgers - Age 5 to 10
- Cadets - age 10 to 16
- LINKS - for those in higher education

Benefits

Being a member of St John Ambulance offers many benefits to children and young people. These include:

- A chance to learn valuable life skills whilst being engaged in fun activities
- Development of social skills
- Increased self-esteem as children achieve a sense of pride and importance when attending public events wearing their uniforms
- It helps children to adopt a more responsible attitude
- Children develop a more caring approach by being involved in their local community

- Volunteer work can lead to further career opportunities for older children and will impress future employers
- LINKS can help students settle into the social side of university more easily when they leave home for the first time

Costs

St John Ambulance usually makes a nominal charge for attending regular meetings, which can be as low as 50p a time and is used towards the upkeep of the building. However, the actual fees vary depending on the particular branch so it is best to check. Uniform is provided free of charge.

How to Find a St John Ambulance Unit

St John Ambulance has a page on its website giving details of its local offices throughout England. This can be viewed at: www.sja.org.uk/sja/about-us/st-john-ambulance-in-your-area.aspx. Alternatively, you should be able to find details of local units in your telephone directory.

Becoming an Adult Volunteer at St John Ambulance

St John Ambulance are looking for volunteer Youth Leaders who help to run weekly meetings for children and young people, train them and arrange social activities. You would have to take part for four or more hours a month and would receive training to enable you to carry out this role. There are also various other volunteering opportunities available for adults. You can find out more information at: www.sja.org.uk/sja/volunteer.aspx.

Chapter 10 - The British Red Cross

Overview

The International Red Cross Movement dates back to 1863 and was started by a Swiss man, Henry Dunant, following the Battle of Solferino in 1859. His idea was to form voluntary societies that provided help to those suffering because of war. As a result of this the International Committee of the Red Cross was established in 1863 in Geneva, and the first Geneva Convention was adopted in 1864.

The British Red Cross (www.redcross.org.uk) originated in 1870 although it wasn't named the British Red Cross until 1905. It followed the Rules of the Geneva Convention and was set up to help soldiers who became sick or wounded as a direct impact of war. In 1907 a network of local branches was set up throughout the country and the Voluntary Aid Scheme began in 1909, ensuring that medical aid was available in wartime.

The Red Cross is well known for its humanitarian and first aid work in disaster areas and war zones but it also provides first aid training, emergency response, and health and social care in the UK as well as overseas. Additionally, it works with refugees and asylum seekers.

There are various opportunities with the Red Cross open to young people from the age of 15. In total, the Red Cross has approximately 70 different volunteer roles as well as offering work experience and internships for young people. Here are some ways in which youngsters can get involved:

Work Experience

Work experience placements are offered for young people from age 15 upwards and it is best to check with the Red Cross for current availability by sending an email to:

workexperience@redcross.org.uk.

These placements are based at locations throughout the country. They last for one to two weeks and give young people the opportunity to learn office skills and find out about how the Red Cross works.

Volunteer Internships

Internships differ from work experience, described in the preceding section, primarily because they last longer. They are usually for between eight and twelve weeks on a part-time basis.

Internships cover a wide variety of activities including: developing projects, carrying out research and organizing events. They are carried out through different departments of the Red Cross, such as: educational engagement - young people, health and social care, international work, fundraising, humanitarian policy and partnerships, refugee services, and marketing and communications. You can find details of current internships offered by checking the website at: www.redcross.org.uk/internships.

Although Internships are on a volunteer basis, expenses for travel and lunch can be claimed.

Shop Volunteers

Volunteer work in Red Cross shops is open to young people from the age of 15, but volunteers must be at least 16 before they can handle money on behalf of the Red Cross. These opportunities give young people practical experience in shop work including: sorting and pricing merchandise, serving customers, operating a cash register and creating displays. As well as practical experience, volunteers can also gain a Certificate in Retail Skills (for those aged under 26) or an NVQ.

To gain a Certificate in Retail Skills young people have to record their progress in a booklet, which is provided by the Red Cross. There are two levels of attainment: the Standard level, which involves about 40 hours of voluntary shop work, and the Advanced Level, which involves about 100 hours of work.

Through participating in the certificate scheme, volunteers can demonstrate the experience they have gained. It also helps them to identify their areas of interest and gain the most out of volunteering as both levels are structured. Each level contains various sections where volunteers learn about different aspects of working in a Red Cross shop. You can find out more at:

www.redcross.org.uk/retailcertificate.

Practical experience in a Red Cross shop can help volunteers to gain an NVQ in retail, which is a more formal, well recognised qualification. It usually takes between six to nine months to accomplish. There are various levels of NVQs in retail involving different tasks, about which the volunteer has to answer questions. At the top level, retail NVQs can prepare volunteers for a supervisory or management career in retail. You can find out more information at:

www.redcross.org.uk/Get-involved/Our-shops/National-Vocational-Qualifications.

First Aid Volunteers

The Red Cross has emergency response teams, and is used to giving first aid at many events held throughout the country. In order to assist at events volunteers need to be at least 15 years of age although they cannot give first aid until they are 16.

International Youth Volunteering

Through its International Youth Volunteering Programme (IYVP), the Red Cross offers placements abroad to young people from the age of 18 for a period of 8 to 12 months. Applications for current placements should be made via the website.

This type of experience can prove invaluable for young people in giving them a chance to learn about other cultures, and perhaps learn a new language whilst providing valuable help to countries where it is needed. Training is provided but applicants should show a commitment to helping other people and communities. At the end of the placement volunteers receive a certificate demonstrating their achievements. You can find out more information at: www.redcross.org.uk/internationalyouthvolunteering.

Gaining Awards

As well as attaining the various certificates and awards described in the preceding sections, young people can volunteer with the Red Cross as part of their work towards the Duke of Edinburgh's Award, which we cover in chapter 17, and Youth Achievement Awards, which you can find out more about at:

www.youthachievementawards.org/index.aspx. NB Youth Achievement Awards are run by UK Youth, which is a membership organization for other groups involved with young people rather than an organization that deals direct with young people. Therefore, it is not featured in this book.

Young people who have positively affected the lives of others can also be nominated for a Red Cross Humanitarian Citizen Award. These awards cover the categories of fundraising and volunteering, community action and first aid and are given out at an annual award ceremony. You can find more details at:

www.redcross.org.uk/theaward.

Peer Education

This forms a part of the Red Cross humanitarian education programme, which we refer to in the following section, and enables young people to support their peers with learning. For example, they could teach people in their age group about first aid or international humanitarian law. You can find more details at:

www.redcross.org.uk/Get-involved/Volunteer/Volunteering-for-young-people/Peer-education-volunteering.

Activities for Younger Children

There is a minimum age requirement of 15 to volunteer with the Red Cross. However, the Red Cross does offer activities for younger children who are not volunteers. The humanitarian education programme, for example, is for a wide range of ages from 5 to 25 and teaches young people about coping with and responding to crisis. The programme is taught through schools and the Red Cross website has a number of resources that can be downloaded for use in the classroom at:

www.redcross.org.uk/education. These cover topics such as health and humanitarianism, disasters and emergencies, and conflict.

For 13 to 14 year olds there is a section on the website to teach them first aid skills in a fun and informative way as well as a section giving ideas for fundraising. These can be found at:

www.redcross.org.uk/Get-involved/Opportunities-for-young-people/Interesting-stuff-for-13-to-14-year-olds.

Children from the ages of four upwards can take part in the Red Cross dance competition, which takes place between March and July. Dancers of all abilities can enter the competition and the finalists have the chance to perform at the O2 arena in London.

For children from the ages of 10 to 14 the website also has a 'Power of Humanity' section offering eight activities which can be downloaded. This can be found at:

www.redcross.org.uk/Get-involved/Opportunities-for-young-people/Power-of-humanity/Download-the-resource. These activities help children to learn about emergencies and teach them how to become a humanitarian citizen. The activities are made up of modules with the first four teaching children about emergencies and the second four enabling them to learn a new skill, such as fundraising or hand massage. The modules are taught in a fun way through role play, arts and crafts and other enjoyable activities.

Who can join?

Young people from the age of 15 can volunteer with the Red Cross although there are activities that younger children can get involved in. All activities for children and the relevant ages are set out in the preceding section. Here is a summary of the requisite ages for volunteering and work experience:

Work Experience is for young people between the ages of 15 and 18.

Internships are open to anyone aged 15 and over including graduates, those on a gap year, people returning to work or those seeking a career change. Applicants must display a desire for working in the voluntary sector.

<u>International Youth Volunteering</u> is open to applicants between the ages of 18 and 30.

<u>First Aid Volunteering</u> is open to people from the age of 16.

<u>Shop Volunteering</u> is open to young people from the age of 15 but they have to be at least 16 to be able to handle money.

<u>Peer Education</u> is open to young people between the ages of 15 and under 26.

<u>Humanitarian Citizen Awards</u> are for young people under the age of 26.

Adults can also volunteer with the Red Cross - please refer to the last section of this chapter for further details.

Benefits

Being a Red Cross volunteer offers a number of benefits to young people including:

- Gaining an appreciation and empathy for the lives of others
- Valuable training in first aid and other skills
- Work experience including office skills and leadership skills
- Gaining a sense of responsibility
- Opportunities to gain confidence and widen social skills through dealing with people from varying backgrounds

- Attaining qualifications such as an NVQ in retail skills
- Receiving a certificate and reference for completion of Internships
- Attaining awards such as the Duke of Edinburgh's Award or Youth Achievement Awards
- A chance to travel and learn about other cultures (for those from age 18)
- International Youth Volunteering (for those from age 18) can provide the opportunity to learn a new language

Costs

There is no charge for volunteering with the British Red Cross. In fact, volunteers are reimbursed for reasonable food and travel expenses. For International Youth Volunteering, participants are given a monthly stipend and all travel, subsistence and accommodation is paid for by the Red Cross.

How to Find a British Red Cross Branch

The Red Cross has various regional branches as well as shops throughout the UK. Each of their regional offices provides a range of services for the region. You can find your nearest branch at: www.redcross.org.uk/Where-we-work/In-the-UK.
The Red Cross also has many overseas branches. Additionally, there are opportunities to join the Red

Cross online community as they have a blog and a presence on Facebook, Twitter and other social media websites. You can find out more at: www.redcross.org.uk/Get-involved/Join-our-online-community.

Becoming an Adult Volunteer with the British Red Cross

Volunteers play a vital role in the services that the Red Cross offers and any adults can volunteer regardless of their existing skills and experiences (subject to CRB checks). You can also put in the amount of time that is most convenient for you. Adult volunteering covers a number of different areas, for example, emergency response, first aid, health and social care, and educational volunteering (as a school speaker) as well as many other opportunities.

The website has a dedicated section regarding volunteering at:

www.redcross.org.uk/Get-involved/Volunteer.
There are many links on this page giving you a host of information so you can find out what volunteering with the Red Cross is all about before you commit.

Chapter 11 - Emergency Services

Overview

Apart from St John Ambulance and the British Red Cross, which we have covered in the previous two chapters, the other emergency services i.e. the Fire Service and the Police Service also have kids' groups, sometimes called cadets. However, local availability varies throughout the country since each division is run separately. Consequently, you may find that there are no police or fire service kids' groups in certain areas. You can check with your individual fire brigade or police force to find out whether they run a group for children, and we will discuss how to do that in the section headed, 'How to Find an Emergency Services Kids' Group'.

Fire Service Cadets

Although each fire service runs its cadet group separately, you can find a lot of information on the Fire Services Youth Training Association (FSYTA) website at: http://www.fsyta.org.uk/.

The FSYTA is a central body for Fire Service Cadet schemes in the UK and its objective is to improve the efficiency of these schemes. Volunteer Fire Cadet schemes are well established in the UK with the first one being founded in 1942. The FSYTA was formed in 1995 following the rapid growth of

Fire Service Cadet schemes during the 1980s and early 1990s, and is a registered charity.

Its functions include the training of young volunteers as well as developing policies and procedures for its members, which are usually Fire Service Cadet organizations. It aims to promote the growth of Fire Cadet schemes throughout all regions in the UK and is an approved body for carrying out CRB checks. The FSYTA holds two national camps a year when cadets from all over the country have a chance to meet. During the camps many competitions take place amongst different cadet units as well as a host of other activities.

Through the FSYTA, Fire Service Cadets have an opportunity to gain qualifications. These include a BTEC Level 2 in Fire and Rescue Services in the community, certificates in adult literacy and numeracy, and a Basic Expedition Leader Award.

Although there is not a cadet group in every part of the country, they are widespread and there are currently more than forty. Please refer to our later section for details of how to find your nearest group.

Each group is run separately although they come under the guidance of the FSYTA. Therefore, the types of activities, meeting times, costs and other details will vary, but we have looked at the Greater Manchester Community Fire Cadets as an example to get a flavour of what is involved. You can find the website at:

www.manchesterfire.gov.uk/community_work/fire_cadets.aspx.

Greater Manchester Fire Service Cadets (Community Fire Cadets) meet one evening a week for two hours at a specified Fire Station. The meetings take the form of a structured educational scheme, which runs for two years, and cadets wear a uniform. The aim of the scheme is to educate young people using Fire and Rescue activities as a basis for developing a range of skills and personal qualities. These include such aspects as mental, physical and social development, self-discipline, Fire Safety and fundraising. The Community Fire Cadets (CFCs) follow a syllabus which is geared towards attainment of a national BTEC qualification in Fire and Rescue Services in the Community. Practical areas of the syllabus include: operational practice, life skills, fire knowledge and fire brigade history amongst others.

Police Service Cadets

The term Police Cadet Scheme used to refer to a full-time paid position with the police for young people, which was similar to an apprenticeship. However, this scheme ceased to exist in England and Wales during the period between 1990 and 1995 although it still exists in Scotland.

Nowadays, the term Police Cadet refers to a volunteer youth organization, which exists in some areas of the UK but not in others. The current cadet groups, called Volunteer Police Cadets (VPCs) started cropping up in various boroughs following the cessation of the former Police Cadet Scheme. They are usually backed financially by a statutory police service although they are run as separate organizations.

Volunteer Police Cadet schemes can give youngsters an insight of what it is like to be in the police, and young people will typically be involved in activities such as crime prevention. Some forces allow young people from the age of 16 to go out with police officers or PCSO's providing the duties are non-confrontational. However, activities will differ from scheme to scheme. Some groups wear uniforms whereas some don't. Again this depends on the individual group or scheme.

The largest cadet scheme in the country is run by the Metropolitan Police Service, London. This scheme is well provided for with its own Police Cadet Training Centre. Here young people learn about the police service, become involved in special attachments and community projects, and learn first aid. The website for the Metropolitan Police Service - Volunteer Cadets is: www.met.police.uk/cadets/.

The Metropolitan Police Service Cadets normally meet one evening a week; many units have additional expeditions including a summer camp. A lot of physical activities take place but these are all checked to ensure that they comply with Health and Safety and Child Protection requirements. Cadets with the Metropolitan Police Service also have the opportunity to gain qualifications and awards in the form of a BTEC in public services and the Duke of Edinburgh's Award.

Who can join?

Fire Service Cadets - We have used the Greater Manchester Community Fire Cadets as an example as each cadet group is run separately. Therefore, it is best to check with your nearest cadet group, but as a typical example the age of entry for Greater Manchester is from 14 up to the age of 17. After the age of 17 it is possible for some young people to become Junior Instructors, and at the age of 18 they could become Volunteer Instructors. Membership at Greater Manchester is open to young people from all backgrounds, abilities and ethnic groups, and both sexes.

Police Cadets - Volunteer Police Cadet (VPC) youth organizations are usually open to young people from the ages of 14 to 18, but for some forces the qualifying age is from 16 to 18, and with the Metropolitan Police Service, London, the age of entry is 14-19. Your local scheme will be able to let you know their requirements.

The Metropolitan Police Service - Volunteer Police Cadets scheme, which is the biggest in the country, states that it is open to anyone meeting the requisite age requirements regardless of background or financial circumstances.

Benefits

Both the Fire Service Cadet and the Volunteer Police Cadet (VPC) schemes provide a wide range of benefits for young people including:

- Gaining a practical insight into how the emergency services operate, which helps with future career decisions
- Developing leadership skills
- Developing an appreciation of the local community
- A chance to experience adventure
- An opportunity to learn valuable skills
- Being involved in something worthwhile in a disciplined environment
- Earning respect and gaining self-confidence
- A chance to take part in competitive and team building events
- Helping to keep fit and healthy through physical activities

- Receiving specialised training and qualifications, which can help future career prospects

Costs

Fire Service - The actual costs are not published on the FSYTA website. However, we checked with the Greater Manchester Fire Cadets who advised that there is no membership or weekly attendance charge for young people who want to become Fire service Cadets, and uniforms are provided. This may vary at other branches in the UK so it is best to contact the branch nearest to you for full details.

Police Service - Costs are usually low as the Police Cadets is a voluntary organization. These costs cover the expense of operating the units. Fees are usually collected in the form of weekly subscriptions and will vary in amount from unit to unit. Often cadets will not need to bring any additional equipment and many units provide a uniform free of charge.

How to Find an Emergency Services Kids' Group

Fire Service - The FSYTA has details of schemes operating throughout the country on a dedicated web page at:

www.fsyta.org.uk/index.php?option=com_brigade&view=brigades&Itemid=97.

Police Service - You can find a list of Police Cadet schemes at:

http://en.wikipedia.org/wiki/Police_cadets_in_the_United_Kingdom#Schemes_in_operation. If your area is not listed on Wikipedia it is worthwhile checking with your local police force as they may have a new cadet scheme in operation or may be planning one for the future. You can find a list of UK police forces at:

www.police.uk/?view=force_sites.

Becoming Involved as a Parent

Fire Service - The Fire Service has a wide variety of positions available to adults, some of which are voluntary and some of which are on a paid basis. These include: support roles (for non-uniformed staff in various departments), full-time Fire-fighters, retained Fire-fighters (who operate on a part-time basis), and roles which involve working with young people to educate them about prevention of fire crime and anti-social behaviour.

You can check with your local Fire Service to find out what positions are available to you. There is a list of Fire Services in the UK, which can be accessed alphabetically at:

www.fireservice.co.uk/information/ukfrs. You can also find out more information on becoming a Fire Service volunteer at:

www.voluntaryworker.co.uk/volunteer-with-your-local-fire-service.html.

Police Service - Adults over the age of 18 can apply to become a Special Constable, which entails working on a part-time basis for a minimum of four hours a week. This is a volunteer position that most people undertake in addition to their full-time job. Although Special Constables are not paid they do receive expenses and a free uniform. Many people join the police as a Special Constable for the experience or to help their local community. You can find out more about becoming a Special Constable at:

http://policerecruitment.homeoffice.gov.uk/special-constables/index.html.

Chapter 12 - Sports Clubs

Overview

Sports clubs are popular with children (and their parents) for a number of reasons: they are widely available, they cover a broad spectrum, children get the chance to meet other children, they help children to keep fit and burn off excess energy, and lastly, because they are fun.

Apart from the wide range of clubs that are available for particular sports it is worthwhile noting that sports and games can form a part of the activities offered by many of the organizations covered in other chapters in this book. For example, local authority holiday schemes may offer a sporting programme through a Sports Trust and the Boys' and Girls' Brigade, Girl Guides and Scouts may offer some sports and games as part of their agenda.

In addition, sports are offered by many bodies in both the public and private sectors. Some sports may have their own associations with a network of affiliated clubs, and other sports may be part of a national drive to produce sporting champions of the future. Therefore, sports such as swimming and gymnastics have a programme of awards, medals and attainment that children can work towards under the guidance of a fully qualified coach. It is worthwhile considering whether you want your child to take part in a sport purely for pleasure or to take part in competitions and win medals and awards. This will greatly affect the amount of time and effort that your child would have to devote to their chosen sport or sports.

There are so many sports to choose from that it would be possible to write a whole book on that subject alone. However, the purpose of this book is to act as an overview of the types of clubs and organizations that are available for children and to give you ideas, inspiration and sources of further information. Here are some sports that you may consider, but you may even think of more:

Football * Swimming * Sailing * Gymnastics *
Tennis * Cricket * Rugby * Athletics * Table
Tennis * Fencing * Diving * Water Sports * Yoga *
Squash * Badminton * Martial Arts * Trampolining
* Ice Skating * Skiing * Cycling * Swimming *
Multi-sports * Basketball * Baseball * Rounders *
Netball * Horse Riding * Pony Trekking *
Canoeing* Polo * Water Polo * Hockey

Who can join?

There are sports to cater for all ages, and some start from as young as two or three although these will usually be of the 'multi-sports' type that introduce children to the concept of taking part in a variety of sports. You may even find groups such as 'Tumble

Tots', which takes very young children (from the age of six months) and introduces them to physical activity using a range of equipment that is specifically tailored to the child's age group. You can find out more about Tumble Tots at:

www.tumbletots.com.

Each sports club or association will have its own rules regarding membership and qualifying ages. Some clubs will have several classes based on age or ability. It is best to check with the particular club or association for their guidelines.

Benefits

There are many benefits of being involved in sports; here are some of them:

- It helps children to stay fit and healthy
- It improves social skills as children meet others with similar interests
- For group sports children learn to work as part of a team
- Many sports help to develop motor skills, co-ordination, balance, agility and flexibility
- Certain sports can help physically disabled children to be mobile e.g. swimming
- Children get a sense of achievement by taking part in something they are good at
- Attainment awards incentivise children and help to improve their self-esteem

Costs

Costs vary tremendously from club to club, but as a guideline, public bodies will usually offer sports at cheaper costs than private clubs. It is best to enquire with the actual club. When thinking about costs, don't forget to factor in any additional expenses, such as sports kit and equipment, competition entry fees, costs of awards and medals, and transport costs to competitions, matches and events.

How to Find a Sports Club

A good starting point is your local authority as many have a sporting programme or a database of local sports clubs so they can advise you what is available in your area. Many local authorities also have a Sports Trust, which combines the services of local authority venues offering sports, such as sports centres, swimming pools and schools. Another good source of information is your local library, which should also keep lists of available clubs and groups.

Sports centres hold a variety of classes for different sports as do private leisure clubs some of which operate as part of hotel chains. You will also find many private groups run by individuals who are qualified in their field, such as football coaches. These will often use public areas such as school fields or church halls, or community centres in the case of indoor sports. Many of these types of clubs or groups send out leaflets to schools advertising their services or post them house to house.

If your town is fortunate enough to have a professional sports club, such as a football, cricket or rugby club, you may find that it offers lessons to children so it is worthwhile making enquiries. A lot of sports will have national bodies that have a database of member clubs so you should be able to find out through them if there is a club in your area.

Another way of finding sports clubs is to enter the name of your child's chosen sport in an Internet search engine together with the name of your town or city and see what results you get. Alternatively, you could try your telephone directory. These searches may also help you to find any national bodies for particular sports.

Becoming Involved as a Parent

Most sports are run by professionals who are qualified to teach the sport so you may find less opportunities to get involved as a parent helper than you would do with other activities. However, you may find a few clubs willing to take parent helpers if you ask. Another alternative, if you want to get involved, is to find a sport or class that teaches parents together with children. For example, some leisure clubs offer classes that both parents and children can participate in, such as karate.

103

Chapter 13 - Animals and Pets

Overview

There are a number of ways in which your children can become involved with animals apart from through owning their own pets. Horse riding lessons is one option although it is expensive. We will cover this option in further detail below.

You will find lots of groups involved in the care of animals. These include children's farms, and groups concerned with wildlife, such as nature reserves, animal rescue centres and animal sanctuaries. Many of these are open to children as well as adults. Children can also become involved in the adoption of pets through schemes run by zoos and other places concerned with animal care.

Horses

As well as learning to ride, some stables will provide lessons on how to look after a horse including stable management, grooming etc. Anything involving horses is very expensive with lessons costing from about £20 for a one hour group riding lesson. Individual private lessons are a lot more expensive. If you decide to keep your own horse this will work out even more costly; as well as the purchase price of the horse, you will need somewhere to keep it and will need to pay for hay, straw, vaccinations, riding gear, saddle etc.

However, if your child attends riding lessons some stables and riding schools will let you hire hats to start with and you can then buy equestrian equipment later, such as jodhpurs and riding boots, second hand from Ebay, or in the local free press ads. Older children may be able to work at the stables in return for lessons, but not all riding schools allow this and those that do will have a minimum age rule due to employment laws.

Farms

Many farms are open to children. Some are working farms that are open to visitors on certain days; others are specifically set up to attract families and call themselves children's farms or petting zoos. Here the kids can feed the animals, ride tractors, or ride horses. Some children's farms also have a park or adventure playground and a cafe. This type of activity is more of an occasional day out than a regular weekly event. However, some farms accept volunteers so it is worth enquiring whether you and your children can help out together.

Zoos

Opportunities offered by zoos vary tremendously but on the whole the management at zoos recognise that a lot of their custom comes from families. It is therefore in their best interest to offer additional services that encourage regular family attendance such as an annual membership, which reduces the cost for each visit. Some host children's birthday parties with an animal theme and some even run regular parent and toddler sessions.

Many zoos encourage fundraising events involving schools and will let you have an information pack regarding fundraising. It is worthwhile suggesting involvement in an event of this kind to your child's teacher if your child is passionate about animals. Find out a few details about it first though to make it easier for the school to take part.

Children can do volunteer work at many zoos but they usually have to be over 16. They would be more likely to be involved with events and exhibits rather than handling animals but at least they would be working in the zoo environment.

Membership of a zoo usually entitles you to free entry all year, discounts in zoo shops and sometimes access to other zoos or events. Some zoos have junior memberships but there are age limits so it is best to check. Chester Zoo, for example, offers junior membership for children aged eight and above, which includes additional events such as a summer school.

Animal adoption is available in many zoos. You pay a set fee, which helps fund the upkeep of the zoo. In return you receive an adoption certificate, pictures of your adopted animal, entry tickets, and other goodies, for instance, magazines and stickers.

Animal Rescue Centres and Sanctuaries

The UK has a good number of animal rescue centres and sanctuaries, many of which are run as charities, which means that they need help from volunteers in order to continue their good work. Some cater only for particular animals e.g. a horse sanctuary; some cater for wild animals, some for pets and others for all animals.

A lot of sanctuaries and animal rescue centres have fundraising events that you as a family can get involved in. They also have animal adoption schemes where you pay towards the upkeep of the animal. In return you will typically receive an adoption certificate, photographs, regular updates of how the animal is progressing and a limited number of visits. However, this varies from place to place and each centre offering animal adoption schemes will have its own rules.

The biggest group involved in animal welfare in the UK is the RSPCA, but there are many others in different areas, for example, the Tameside Animal Shelter, which is located in an area of Manchester. Part of the work of the RSPCA is to rescue pets that have been mistreated and provide rehabilitation (and in some cases medical treatment) for them until a permanent home can be found. The organization also rescues and rehabilitates wild animals until they are able to survive in the wild.

The RSPCA has an Animal Action Club for children aged from 7 to 12, which gives them membership of the RSPCA as well as other goodies including magazines, puzzles, stickers etc. There is also a teenage membership for those aged between 12 and 17. Teenage members get involved in fundraising and campaigning on behalf of animals and are given information and advice about helping the RSPCA.

Volunteering is open to older children from the age of 16, rather than younger children due to the health issues involved in handling animals. Nevertheless, there are opportunities for children to get involved with the RSPCA in other ways, such as fundraising, so it is best to enquire at the local branch for more information. For those aged 16+ volunteering can involve a range of activities including practical animal care, administration and working in RSPCA shops.

Some animal rescue centres may have lower minimum age requirements than the RSPCA. For example, children from the age of 14 can volunteer at Tameside Animal Shelter, although for some animal rescue centres the minimum age may be as old as 18. Others may allow younger children to volunteer as long as they are accompanied by an adult helper. It is best to make enquiries with the centre of your choice.

Nature Reserves

The Wildlife Trust is the biggest voluntary UK organization involved in the protection of all wildlife, with 47 individual Wildlife Trusts, and 800,000 members. Its work involves the protection of wildlife habitats including woodlands, beaches, lakes and moors. This in turn helps the animals that live in those habitats. You can find out more about The Wildlife Trust at: www.wildlifetrusts.org/who-we-are.

150,000 members are juniors, and the junior membership branch is called Wildlife Watch. By joining one of the Wildlife Watch groups children can find out not only about wild animals in the UK, but about their environment in general and how to take care of it. Activities that Wildlife Watch groups take part in are wide-ranging and can include: beach cleans, barn owl surveys, environmental artwork, pond dipping and hands-on conservation work such as tree planting. Wildlife Watch group leaders are assessed to ensure that they are suitable to work with children, and groups operate according to child welfare and safety guidelines.

Meetings take place once a month or more depending on the individual group. This could involve an indoor meeting or a visit to a nature reserve. Some groups encourage involvement by parents, but others prefer parents not to attend all of the group's activities.

Age requirements for membership also depend on the individual group. Some operate a group for under 12s and a group for teenagers whereas others operate groups for those aged over 12 only. The annual membership fee includes lots of goodies, for example, a membership card, handbook, magazines, badge, stickers and an animal poster. Junior members can also take part in award schemes organized by the Wildlife Trusts. There are three different awards, which are The Hedgehog award, the Kestrel award and the Nature Ranger award.

The Hedgehog award is aimed at children under eight who can choose from a list of eight wildlife activities to complete. Through completion of the activities they can collect stamps to earn a special certificate. A hedgehog icon will also be added to their website profile (if they are a registered user of the Wildlife Watch website).

The Kestrel Award is aimed at those over eight and has four wildlife challenges, which are: Create it!, Do it!, Record it! and Shout about it! Once they have completed the challenges they will receive a certificate and badge and the Kestrel icon will be added to their website profile (if they are a registered user of the Wildlife Watch website).

The Nature Ranger award is the highest level Wildlife Watch award. Completing this award requires participants to study a UK wildlife or conservation topic of their choice and to produce a report for their local Wildlife Trust to assess. Once completed, recipients will get a certificate signed by Chris Packham, a badge, an icon on their website profile, a mention in Wildlife Watch magazine and a special prize!

Who can join?

There are opportunities for children of all ages to get involved with animals although visits to farms and zoos may be more appropriate for younger children. Getting them involved in zoo membership, animal adoption schemes and horse riding lessons will be more suitable when children are old enough to understand what this entails or, in the case of horse riding, when they are physically able. Zoo membership age requirements will vary from zoo to zoo, and many horse riding schools will have a minimum age requirement. In the case of animal adoption schemes it is up to your own judgement to decide when your child is ready.

As there is such a wide range of opportunities for children of various ages to get involved with animals, it is difficult to generalise. Therefore, it is always best to enquire at the particular farm, zoo, animal sanctuary or other animal centre whether they have any rules regarding the involvement of children, and whether there are any age stipulations. However, we have given a general guide regarding age requirements for the RSPCA and the Wildlife Trusts in our overview section above.

Benefits

Taking an interest in animals or being involved in the care of them can bring many benefits and rewards to children and their families:

- It can teach children to be responsible, disciplined, and respectful towards other living beings
- Horse riding can teach children about good posture
- It helps children to develop a caring approach
- Children learn about the physical tasks that the care of animals entails
- Children have the satisfaction of knowing that animals benefit from the input of volunteers and fundraisers
- Involvement with outside groups means parents don't necessarily have the inconvenience and expense involved in keeping pets in the home
- Children have the chance to socialise with other children and adults who are also interested in animal care

- Voluntary work can lead to career opportunities working with animals
- Owning a pet can help to improve a child's self-esteem

Costs

These vary enormously and it all depends on the level and type of involvement. Horse riding is likely to be at the higher end of the scale as lessons alone are expensive and then there are all the associated costs to take into account as described above. At the lower end of the scale will be any voluntary work that your child is able to take part in.

There is lots of middle ground when it comes to cost, such as zoo membership, occasional visits to farms and zoos and animal adoption schemes. Fees for all of these will vary from venue to venue and, as a generalisation, the larger the venue, the higher the costs. For example, an animal adoption scheme in a large well-known zoo is likely to be more expensive than one at a small animal sanctuary.

Membership of the RSPCA kids' clubs costs £15 a year for children aged 7 to 12 and £10 a year for teenagers from 12 to 17.

Annual membership of Wildlife Watch usually costs up to £19 for a family of up to four children residing at one address. Membership of Wildlife Watch can also be included as part of a family membership of the Wildlife Trust. Some local groups may make a small charge for attending regular meetings as well. This charge covers such items as room hire, and materials for activities.

How to Find Groups Involving Animals and Pets

Firstly, try entering specific search terms in an Internet search engine, for instance, 'children's horse riding lessons', or 'children's farms'. Alternatively, you could look up these terms in your local telephone directory.

If you want to find out about animal venues in general, a good source of information is at: www.kidsguide.co.uk, which gives details of farms, zoos and animal sanctuaries in different locations.

The website for the RSPCA is: www.rspca.org.uk and you can find further information regarding RSPCA clubs and activities for under 18s at: www.rspca.org.uk/theden.

The Wildlife Trust website is at:

www.wildlifetrusts.org and the Wildlife Watch website is at: www.wildlifewatch.org.uk. All of these websites will contain information regarding their junior membership schemes.

Becoming Involved as a Parent

As explained in the preceding sections, there are many opportunities for parents to work as volunteers at a wide variety of venues that are associated with animals. You may also find that some places allow your children to volunteer only if they are accompanied by an adult. Other places have stricter rules and will not accept child volunteers at all. However, parents can become members of zoos or can contribute to animal adoption schemes on behalf of their children.

Parents can be members of the RSPCA or their local Wildlife Trusts and some groups offer family membership covering parents and children.

Chapter 14 - Local Authority Organized Schemes

Overview

Many local authorities have a range of regular activities and schemes to keep children entertained. These usually involve Sports Trusts, libraries, museums and art galleries, but the pastimes on offer vary tremendously from area to area. Some activities take place on a regular basis, such as weekly swimming lessons at the public swimming pool; others involve schemes that take place during the school holidays, and many boroughs publish a programme specifically for children's events.

Although some boroughs do not cover as wide a variety of activities as others, the following are typical of the types of pastimes that can be offered:

Sports

Many Local Authorities have a sporting programme for children and sports take place either after school and at weekends, or during the school holidays. A number of venues are used including public sports centres, school sports halls and gymnasiums, and public parks. The range of sports on offer varies depending on the Local Authority, which often provides the programme in conjunction with a Sports Trust.

Holiday Play Schemes

These usually take place in schools and other public buildings, and involve a range of games, sports, arts, crafts and other activities catering for various age groups.

Art Galleries

Some Art Galleries hold regular arts and crafts classes with additional classes offered during school holidays.

Libraries

Libraries usually offer reading based activities, such as story time for younger children or visits by children's authors, but you will also find arts and crafts taking place especially during school holidays. A lot of libraries have a Bookstart club aimed specifically at the under fives to encourage them with learning to read.

Museums

You will find a range of themed events, special interest days and holiday activities at museums. Activities can include children's discovery trails and quizzes, for example.

Who can join?

Local Authority activities and schemes are open to all children subject to age stipulations. They normally operate according to set age ranges and will usually state clearly what age range the particular activity is suitable for. Some Authorities will include activities specifically for the under fives in their programme of events as well as pastimes aimed at older children.

Benefits

Specific benefits will depend on the type of activity, but in general terms benefits can include:

- A way in which to engage children during school holidays, making the transition from holidays to term time easier
- Helps children to make more of their free time and stops them becoming bored
- Helps children to learn new skills or enhance existing skills
- Children have a chance to socialise with others who have similar interests
- Events at venues such as museums and art galleries can enhance your children's knowledge
- Involvement in things that they are good at can raise children's self-esteem
- Can alleviate some of the stress suffered by parents during long school holidays
- Participation in sports can help with physical development
- Themed events enable children to embrace important occasions such as Christmas and New Year

- Enables parents to keep tabs on how their children are spending their free time and reduces the temptation for young people to engage in less worthwhile activities

Costs

A distinct advantage with any activity or scheme offered by a local authority is that the cost is really low, with many leisure services being offered free of charge. You will often find that local authorities publish the costs of events in the written programmes that they produce, or on their websites. We will give more details about event programmes in the following section.

How to Find Local Authority Schemes

You can find out about local authority activities and events through the local authority websites. Programmes of events are published by most local authorities and they usually distribute these programmes through local authority buildings, such as libraries, art galleries and museums. Sometimes they will send out programmes as inserts in the local press. It is very useful to get hold of a programme of events as it enables you to plan your kids' school holidays around it.

The Direct Gov website has a search facility that enables you to find your nearest local authority. You can find this facility at:

http://local.direct.gov.uk/LDGRedirect/index.jsp?L GSL=18&LGIL=8. This will enable you to find out about your local school holiday scheme, and any other children's clubs run by your local authority, by firstly finding your local authority's website or contact details.

Some local authorities will run separate schemes for different types of activity. So, for example, the Sports Trust may publish a leaflet for sports, and art galleries and museums may publish a separate leaflet for events that take place at the various art galleries and museums in the borough.

Programmes or leaflets may be dedicated to children in particular, or to school holiday schemes. Alternatively, activities for children may form part of a larger booklet that also encompasses authority run activities and events in general. Sometimes you can get hold of booklets that cover all events and activities in the borough for a particular season, which are often set out in date order or under different headings.

Becoming Involved as a Parent

Some local authority schemes require the attendance of an adult whereas with others you leave the children in their care and pick them up later. For all-day events such as holiday sports programmes, you normally have to provide a packed lunch, so it is best to check with the particular scheme whether this is a requirement.

Chapter 15 - Arts and Crafts

Overview

Involvement in arts and crafts can open up a whole new world of creativity for your children. For those with a creative nature, there is nothing more satisfying than seeing the completion of a piece of work that they have put their little hearts into. Arts and crafts encompass a wide range of activities, including:

Drawing * Painting * Stencilling * Pottery *
Cookery * Baking * Needlecrafts * Weaving *
Collage Work * Clay Modelling * Cutting * Gluing
* Printing * Colouring In * Card Making * Papier
Mache * Model Making * Puppet Making * Bead
Work * Mask Making * Badge Making

In the preceding chapter we have given details of arts and crafts clubs that are run by local authorities, libraries and art galleries. However, you can find a range of arts and crafts in other sectors including privately run groups dedicated to arts and crafts, and shops that offer classes as well as selling materials. Some of these art groups and shops may be small local ones, but here are a couple of larger, national groups offering arts and crafts for children:

Hobbycraft (www.hobbycraft.co.uk)

Hobbycraft stores regularly hold events, some of which are suitable for children. They are usually tied to celebrations or occasions rather than being a regular weekly club. Many of the events are free of charge and enable children to take home any crafts that they have made. The events vary from store to store, but you can find details of what is happening at your local Hobbycraft store by selecting the relevant store at:

www.hobbycraft.co.uk/Pages/Stores/. Once you have clicked on the relevant store from the drop down list you will see contact details and opening hours as well as a list of events taking place at that store.

The Creation Station

(www.thecreationstation.co.uk/)

There are numerous branches of the Creation Station throughout the UK; you can find your nearest branch at:

http://thecreationstation.co.uk/Franchise-Map/. The group was founded by a mum of three who has an Art Management Diploma and had previously worked in a disabled centre as the Head of Art and Photography. She spent five years developing the arts and crafts sessions in accordance with the Department of Education's framework for the Early Years Foundation Stage (EYFS). This means that the sessions for under 5s help to prepare them for school.

The Creation Station has regular sessions for different age groups from babies to children aged up to 11, as well as family classes during school holidays. It also offers party packages with fully trained children's party entertainers.

Apart from the numerous branches of the Creation Station that can be found in the UK, the company works with local councils, children's centres and children's charities as well as many other organizations. So, even if you cannot find a Creation Station in your area, you may be able to access their facilities through one of the organizations that they work with. You can find out more at: www.thecreationstation.co.uk/arts-crafts-groups-events-provider.

Although the Creation Station charges for classes and events, they do offer a free initial Baby Discovery class, and there is a free activities section on the website.

Kiddy Cook (http://kiddycook.co.uk/)

Cookery may not always come under the heading of 'arts and crafts', but nevertheless it is a very creative pastime and a good one to get kids involved in. It also offers many of the same benefits as arts and crafts activities. For example, joining a kids' cookery club gives children the chance to interact with others, builds their confidence and enables them to derive a sense of satisfaction from seeing the end result of their input. In addition, kids' cookery classes encourage children to take an interest in food and healthy eating.

Kiddy Cook offers a range of children's cookery classes for children from the ages of two to eleven. Cookie Tots is aimed at children aged from two to four years and takes place weekly during term time. During classes parents help their children to cook using simple recipes. Other activities take place during classes, which revolve around cooking; these include music and games.

Kiddy Cook classes are for those aged four plus. During Kiddy Cook sessions children find out about food and how it is created through involvement in the entire cookery process. This means that they will work from a recipe and will be weighing and measuring ingredients.

Apart from the above classes Kiddy Cook hosts children's parties involving activities based around cookery at a venue provided by the parents. Kiddy Cook also provides healthy eating and cookery workshops within schools, and Pick and Cook workshops in partnership with the National Trust, farms and allotments. Through these workshops children learn where food comes from and are taught how to pick and prepare that food.

Kiddy Cook currently has 19 branches throughout England. However, it is a growing business, which operates on a franchise basis, and is offering franchise opportunities throughout the UK.

Who can join?

The classes and groups described above are open to all children subject to costs and age requirements. Please refer to specific groups in the preceding section for age requirements, and to our later section on costs.

Benefits

Apart from giving children hours of enjoyment and exploring their creative side, arts and crafts classes can also offer the following benefits:

- They help to improve your children's self-confidence
- They can improve social skills as children make friends with others in the class
- They develop children's hand-eye co-ordination
- They enable children to see their ideas materialise
- Children have the opportunity to practice problem solving skills
- Children learn to carry out instructions
- They help children with decision making
- They can improve levels of concentration
- Parents are able to engage with their children in a fun way

- Parents and children can pick up ideas to try outside the class
- Interaction at classes helps with speech development

Costs

You will find that groups operated by your local authority, library or art gallery will be the cheapest option. These often just ask for a small contribution towards art materials and some are even free. Prices for all other groups will vary so it is best to check with the group of your choice.

How to Find an Arts and Crafts Club

A good starting point for finding groups in your area is always with your local authority or library. You can find details of your local authority at: www.direct.gov.uk/en/Dl1/Directories/Localcouncil s/AToZOfLocalCouncils/DG_A-Z_LG, and public libraries will usually provide information over the counter.

For private clubs, we have given details of a couple of larger ones in our 'overview' section, with website addresses. You can also try finding other groups in your area by looking up 'arts and crafts clubs (+ your area)' in an Internet search engine or try searching in your telephone directory. You can also try local arts and crafts shops to see if they offer art classes for children or if they know of anywhere that does.

Becoming Involved as a Parent

In many instances you will be able to attend arts and crafts classes with your children; in fact, for younger children the attendance of a parent is likely to be a requirement since your children will need help with the activities.

If you really want to be involved with arts and crafts on a professional level, both the Creation Station and Kiddy Cook operate on a franchise basis and they are currently looking for new franchisees. You can find more information relating to Creation Station franchises via the website at:

www.thecreationstation.co.uk/become-a-franchisee/,

and relating to Kiddy Cook franchises at:

http://kiddycook.co.uk/franchises.

Chapter 16 - The Cadet Forces

Overview

These comprise of the Army Cadets, Sea Cadets and Air Cadets, and are aimed at young people who enjoy taking part in challenging activities. Although they have connections with the armed forces they all operate as separate bodies from them. The Army Cadet Force states that there is no military call up for its members as they do not belong to the army although they are sponsored by it. The Sea Cadets organization also stresses that it is not a recruiter for the armed forces, and the Air Cadet Organization states that it does not recruit for the RAF, but it does give a head start to those that are interested in a career in the Armed Forces.

Army Cadets

The Army Cadet Force (ACF) is a voluntary organization which is now more than 150 years old, and it has in excess of 45,000 cadets in 1700 detachments throughout the UK. It provides a wide variety of activities that help young people to develop physically, socially and intellectually. These activities are exciting, adventurous and challenging whilst also being educational. Some have a military basis but others focus on the community, and this combination gives tremendous scope for personal development. Typical activities include: abseiling, mountain biking, archery and rock climbing.

Meetings usually take place twice weekly in the evenings, but there are also some weekend events, for instance, camping and sports competitions, as well as an annual summer camp. This trip is of one to two weeks duration and takes place at a military training area in the UK. The annual camp usually costs less than £100 including food, transport and accommodation.

Army Cadets have the opportunity to earn qualifications such as the Duke of Edinburgh's Award or a BTEC Diploma as well as the Army Proficiency Certificate. The latter consists of a course that is followed by all Army Cadets who work towards various levels. The top level is Master Cadet. Each level gets progressively more challenging and enables cadets to develop skills and knowledge in many areas. These include: first aid, military knowledge, drill and turnout, shooting and many more.

All adult volunteers are subject to a CRB check and are not left to supervise cadets alone until the CRB check is complete. The ACF also has a Training Safety Advisor for every branch, who works full-time to ensure that all training is carried out safely.

Sea Cadets and Royal Marines Cadets

The Sea Cadets organization was founded in 1856, and operates in partnership with the Royal Navy. It is a registered charity so it is able to raise funds to help with running costs. There are over 400 Sea Cadet Units in the UK with a total of 14,000 cadets.

The aim of the Sea Cadets is to give young people a good start in life by offering a range of challenging activities with a nautical theme. These help to develop key life skills like team work, leadership and communication.

Sea Cadets have opportunities to take part in many exciting activities and events as well as learning a wide range of useful skills. Activities include: canoeing, sailing, abseiling, shooting and many others. As well as attending regular meetings, Sea Cadets have opportunities to attend training courses and summer camps.

Royal Marines Cadets are part of the Sea Cadets. They take part in the same activities as the Sea Cadets but with the addition of specialist training in areas such as weapon handling and map reading. This additional training is very demanding but rewarding for those seeking a challenge.

The Sea Cadets organization operates a rank structure similar to that operated by the Royal Navy, and cadets progress through the ranks as they gain experience and knowledge. For Royal Marines Cadets the structure is similar to that operated by the Royal Marines. Sea Cadets also have the opportunity to gain many nationally recognised qualifications including: the Duke of Edinburgh's Award, BTEC qualifications, and qualifications from other groups, such as the Royal Yachting Association and the British Canoeing Union.

All volunteer helpers with the Sea Cadets have to have a CRB check and the Sea Cadets organization works in conjunction with CEOP (Child Exploitation and Online Protection) to make certain that cadets are kept safe. Qualified instructors also carry out risk assessments on all Sea Cadet activities.

Air Cadets

The Air Cadet Organization has over 40,000 members who are aged from 13 to 20, with older members joining the Volunteer Section rather than the cadets. It dates back to 1859 when the first organizations were formed in schools, but it wasn't until the 1930s that the RAF section of the Combined Cadet Force began, and 1938 when the Air Defence Cadet Corps (now known as the Air Training Corps) was established.

The Air Cadet Organization is sponsored by the Royal Air Force and, therefore, one of its aims is to promote an interest in the Royal Air Force and in aviation in general amongst its members. However, this isn't the Air Cadets' only focus; the skills that it teaches can also be useful outside the Air Force, such as leadership and good citizenship.

In the present day the Air Cadet Organization has two sections: the Air Training Corps and the Combined Cadet Force. The Air Training Corps has over 900 squadrons throughout the UK. The Combined Cadet Force (CCF) comprises of cadets from the Air Cadets, Army Cadets and Sea Cadets, and the Air Cadet section of this is called the CCF (RAF). The CCF is active in more than 200 UK schools.

Some of the activities that Air Cadets become involved in include: taking part in aircraft flights, sports, shooting, music and abseiling, as well as many more. Air Cadets also have opportunities to take part in adventure camping trips and sometimes go abroad. The Air Cadet Organization also runs a Summer Leadership course, which teaches leadership skills.

Air Cadets progress through a series of ranks, from Junior Cadet to Master Air Cadet, as they gain experience and skills. There are also opportunities for Air Cadets to gain qualifications and awards, such as the Duke of Edinburgh's Award, various BTEC courses and a City and Guilds qualification in management.

All adult volunteers with the Air Cadet Organization are CRB checked as well as undergoing internal security checks prior to being put in sole charge of cadets. Furthermore, they receive training in the safety aspects of their role as well as training for any activities they are involved in.

Who can join?

Army Cadets - Boys or girls from the ages of 12 to 18 can join the Army Cadets. Children must also be in year eight at school as a minimum. There are no membership restrictions in terms of ability or background.

Sea Cadets - Boys and girls aged from 10 to 18 can join the Sea Cadets. Each unit is divided into two, with Junior Cadets aimed at those aged from 10 to 12 and Sea Cadets for those aged from 12 to 18.

Air Cadets - The Air Cadets is open to young people from the ages of 13 to 17. However, young people who are older than 17 can join the Volunteer Section.

Benefits

Army Cadets, Sea Cadets and Air Cadets all have a number of benefits for young members, some of which are:

- They train young people in how to become good citizens
- Children learn how to work as part of a team

- Children receive valuable cadet training
- They encourage young people to become responsible and self-reliant, and to use their initiative
- Children develop leadership skills
- It enhances children's communication skills as they interact with others in a fun, exciting and challenging environment
- They open up a range of new experiences and opportunities to young people
- There are opportunities to gain vocational qualifications
- They foster a desire to be successful in life
- They give young people a sense of purpose and can help them to stay out of trouble
- Experience as a cadet can pave the way for a career in the armed services
- The skills and qualifications gained also help in civilian careers

Costs

Army Cadets – The cost for attendance at regular meetings is very low, usually between 50p and £1.00 a time. Uniforms are provided free of charge whilst the young person is a cadet, but there may be a small deposit to pay. Parents will need to buy a good pair of boots for their child.

Sea Cadets - Most units ask for a small donation from cadets and the amount varies depending on the unit. Trips and camps are charged separately with all costs being kept to a minimum. There is no charge to cadets for uniforms as these are provided by the unit.

Air Cadets - Uniform is provided and, as this is worth about £200, the Air Cadet Organization stresses that it must be well looked after. They do not supply footwear so you will need to provide a pair of shoes or boots. Much of the Air Cadet activities are funded by the RAF, but they do ask for a small donation of about £10 per month to help towards costs. Camps and trips are charged as extra but the Air Cadet Organization tries to keep the costs as low as possible.

How to Find a Local Group

Army Cadets has a facility on its website to enable you to find your nearest detachment. The relevant page of the website is: http://armycadets.com/find-a-detachment/.

Sea Cadets has a 'Sea Cadets Unit Finder' on its website, which you can access at:

www.sea-cadets.org/find-your-nearest-unit-4.aspx.

Air Cadets has a page on its website that enables you to find your nearest squadron. You can find the page at: www.raf.mod.uk/aircadets/findasquadron/.

Becoming Involved as a Parent

Army Cadets – The Army Cadet Force takes adult volunteers from the age of 18 upwards, and it currently has 8,500 volunteers. You don't have to have any experience and will be given training to carry out your duties. However, you will have to undergo a CRB check before you can work with cadets unsupervised. To find out more about becoming a volunteer take a look at:

http://armycadets.com/volunteer-with-us/.

Sea Cadets - The Sea Cadets relies on volunteers to run its activities and there are 9,000 volunteers in the UK. There are a variety of roles to suit specific skills, but the Sea Cadets also offers training. To become a volunteer with the Sea Cadets you will have to have a CRB check. You can find out more about volunteering with the Sea Cadets at: www.sea-cadets.org/volunteer.aspx.

Air Cadets - The Air Cadet Organization is looking for adult volunteers from the age of 20 upwards. Adult members receive training and also have opportunities to gain qualifications. Volunteers should be physically fit and have the patience to work with young people as well as an understanding of their needs. Obviously, as a parent, you will qualify in that area. There are various opportunities available for adults and you can find out more at:

www.raf.mod.uk/aircadets/wanttojoin/adultvolunteers.cfm.

Chapter 17 - The Duke of Edinburgh's Award

Overview

The Duke of Edinburgh's (DofE) Award is the leading achievement award in the world in relation to young people. It began in 1956 with the Duke of Edinburgh as the Chairman, but it was only open to boys initially. It opened up to girls in 1958. Since that time it has grown and developed at a tremendous rate, and in 2011, 79,000 young people gained an award.

The DofE programme is run as a charity and receives donations from businesses. There are currently three awards that can be obtained, which are the Bronze Award, the Silver Award and the Gold Award. These are open to specific age groups, which are covered in the next section.

There are over 10,000 centres that hold meetings relating to The Duke of Edinburgh's Award. These are a mix of youth clubs, schools, colleges, voluntary organizations, businesses and others. The centres are supported by over 400 Licensed Organizations, and are not just based in the UK but all over the world. DofE staff are trained to a high level and child safety aspects are included in their training. However, depending on the activities that your child becomes involved in, some of these may not come under the direct supervision of the DofE centre. For example, your child may want to help out at local fitness classes or at an animal shelter as part of the volunteering section of his award. Therefore, you should bear child safety aspects in mind and make sure that the activity is suitably managed and supervised.

The Duke of Edinburgh's Award is designed to develop young people in three areas referred to as, 'mind, body and soul'. The programme works in conjunction with many other organizations, some of which have been referred to throughout this book. These include: the Boys Brigade, the Girls Brigade, The Scout Association, British Red Cross, Police Cadets, Cadet Forces and many more.

Participants usually start working at the easiest level, which is the Bronze Award, as the levels become progressively more difficult, with the Gold Award being the most demanding. However, as there are specific age requirements for each award, young people who join at a later stage may want to start at a more advanced level. In terms of the structure of the awards, the Bronze, Silver and Gold Awards each comprise of distinct sections with different timescales, as follows:

Bronze Award

- Volunteering - Participants must spend at least three months on this activity.

- <u>Physical</u> - Participants must spend at least three months on this activity.

- <u>Skills</u> - Again participants must spend at least three months on a skills related activity.

- <u>Expedition</u> - The expedition lasts for two days and one night but participants will have to plan and train for this activity and they usually have a practice expedition beforehand.

In addition to these four sections participants have to spend an extra three months on either the volunteering, physical or skills-based activity. Therefore, the activities relating to the Bronze Award usually last a total of six months.

<u>Silver Award</u>

- <u>Volunteering</u> - Participants have to spend at least six months on this activity.

- <u>Physical</u> - Participants must spend at least six months on this activity and three months on a skills-based activity, or three months on this activity and six months on a skills based activity.

- <u>Skills</u> - Participants must spend at least six months on this activity and three months on a physical activity, or three months on this activity and six months on a physical activity.

- Expedition - the expedition lasts for three days and two nights and participants have to plan and train for it as they do with the Bronze Award.

If participants have not already gained their Bronze Award then they will have to spend an additional six months on either their volunteering activity, or the physical or skills based activity that they have already elected to spend six months on. Therefore, it will normally take six months to gain a Silver Award for young people who already have a Bronze Award. For those who take part in the Silver Award without having first gained the Bronze Award it will take a minimum of twelve months.

Gold Award

- Volunteering - Candidates must spend 12 months on this activity.

- Physical - Candidates must spend either 12 months on a physical activity and 6 months on a skills-based activity, or vice versa.

- Skills - Candidates must spend either 12 months on a skills-based activity and 6 months on a physical activity or vice versa.

- Expedition - The expedition takes place over four days and three nights and it has to be in 'wild' country. Participants will also have an 'acclimatisation' day.

- Residential - For the Gold Award participants will also attend a residential for five days and four nights. During this time they will take part in a shared activity with other people that they will meet during the residential.

If participants haven't already gained their Bronze and Silver Awards they will have to spend an additional six months on either volunteering, or the physical or skills-based activity that they have already elected to do for an initial 12 months. It normally takes a minimum of 12 months to gain the Gold Award or 18 months if the participant hasn't already gained the Silver Award.

It is up to the participants to select the activities that they want to get involved in for each section of their Duke of Edinburgh's Award, with the exception of the expedition and residential sections. The expedition activity usually takes place under the guidance of one or more supervisors; you can find more details at:

www.dofe.org/en/content/cms/doing-your-dofe/activities-sections/expedition/.

For the residential section the participant will have a choice, but all residential activities have to take place with an Approved Activity Provider, registered charity or other organized group. You can find more details of requirements for this section at: www.dofe.org/en/content/cms/doing-your-dofe/activities-sections/residential/residential-require/.

The Duke of Edinburgh's Award website has a comprehensive list of ideas for activities relating to the voluntary, skills and physical sections, as well as points to consider regarding which activity to choose. Additionally, activities have to be deemed suitable by the Licensed Organization so it is wise to run through any ideas with the DofE Centre Leader. You can find more information about choosing activities at:

www.dofe.org/en/content/cms/doing-your-dofe/activities-sections/. This page of the website also leads to sub-pages giving details of what is involved in the activities relating to each section of the Duke of Edinburgh's Award.

When your child joins a Duke of Edinburgh's Award programme he will get access to an online area of the DofE website where he will record his activities. This will need to be kept up to date as evidence of his involvement to enable him to qualify for an award.

<u>Who can join?</u>

The Duke of Edinburgh's Award programme is open to all young people from the ages of 14 to 24 regardless of their background. Each of the awards has specific age requirements, as follows:

Bronze Award - usually from the age of 14, or almost 14.

Silver Award - Usually from the age of 15 but participants may be allowed to start working towards their award when they are almost 15 provided they have already earned their Bronze Award.

Gold Award - Strictly from the age of 16.

All activities relating to any of these awards must be completed before the participant's 25th birthday.

Benefits

The benefits of gaining a Duke of Edinburgh's Award and of taking part in the various activities are numerous. These include:

- A chance to receive an award that is looked upon favourably by employers and universities
- Encouragement to take part in voluntary work
- Increased self-esteem and confidence
- Improved ability in sports and physical activity
- Increased levels of fitness
- Opportunities to try out new and exciting activities

- A positive impact on young people in custody
- Development of a more caring nature and a willingness to help others
- A chance to gain new skills
- Young people become more responsible
- A chance to make new friends
- Development of leadership skills
- Development of team working and problem solving skills
- Practising time management skills
- Development of presentation skills

Costs

Because the Duke of Edinburgh's Award programme operates as a charity, costs are usually very low, and any fees paid contribute towards the running of the programme. You will have to provide some of the kit that is required for expeditions, such as sturdy walking boots and warm waterproof clothing, but many of the other more expensive items can be borrowed from The Duke of Edinburgh's centres, i.e. backpacks and tents. Participants can also receive discounts on kit items through The Duke of Edinburgh's programme. Details of how to obtain discounts can be found at: www.dofe.org/en/content/cms/life-zone/commercial-partners/expedition-kit-list/.

How to Find a Local Centre

To find your nearest DofE centre you need to get in touch with the Licensed Organization for your region. You can find details of DofE Licensed Organizations throughout the UK at:

www.dofe.org/takepart/.

Becoming Involved as a Parent

Ways in which you can support your child are by helping and encouraging him to record his progress online, giving him lifts to DofE centres or other locations where his activities take place, and supplying any necessary equipment.

You could also become involved as a volunteer and help out in other ways, for example, administration, driving a minibus or giving guidance and help to young people. You do not need any qualifications initially but if you become a regular volunteer you will need to go through standard checks. The DofE also offers a high level of training for volunteers to assist them in carrying out various roles. You can find out more about volunteer opportunities at: www.dofe.org/en/content/cms/leaders/volunteer-roles/.

Chapter 18 - The Prince's Trust

Overview

Many people probably connect The Prince's Trust with the provision of finance for young people starting in business, but this is only one aspect of their work. The Prince's Trust is a charity that has the specific aim of helping young people from the ages of 13 to 30. This charity works in particular with disadvantaged young people, such as the long-term unemployed, those in care, those who have struggled in school and young offenders. The Prince's Trust offers a number of programmes aimed at different age groups and situations. These age groups are detailed under our section 'Who can join?', and the programmes are, as follows:

Team Programme

This programme is aimed primarily at unemployed young people although a few employed people take part as well. It is a twelve week course that aids young people in acquiring skills that can help them find employment. The course includes a community based project, a team challenge that entails caring for others, a week spent at a residential activity centre, a work placement and a group presentation at the end of the course based on experiences gained from the programme. Participants also develop a post programme plan to help with their futures.

The scheme has been in operation since 1990 and has had a high success rate. Over 70% of participants gain employment, or go on to further training or education, within three months of finishing the programme.

Fairbridge Programme

This is a personal development programme aimed at young people who are disengaged for a variety of reasons including: homelessness, a history of offending or substance abuse. The course offers these young people positive experiences and valuable skills enabling them to re-engage in society. The programme is delivered using a combination of one to one learning and group activities. It is currently being run at 15 Prince's Trust Centres in the UK, which are situated in the most disadvantaged areas.

Participants start the programme with a five day access course, which consists of challenging, adventurous activities and usually entails spending a few days at an outdoor residential centre. They then choose to follow a pathway which suits them and are supported with their personal development throughout the course. This includes support with moving on to other positive pathways, such as education, training or employment once the participant is ready to take the next step. Although

Fairbridge used to be a separate organization it is now part of The Prince's Trust.

Get into…

These are vocational courses that help young people to develop the skills that will assist them in gaining employment. The courses are developed in partnership with local businesses in order to meet the employment demands in the area. Types of careers that are covered include: construction, customer services, retail, hospitality, logistics and cooking. Success rates after completing the course are high with 50% of young people going on to employment and 25% going on to further training. Duration of the courses is from between two to six weeks and participants can gain qualifications suited to their particular career choice. On completion of the course participants are also given further support to help them find employment or further training opportunities.

Get Started

This short course lasts between five and eight days and aims to engage young people through sport or the performing arts. This helps to increase the confidence of the participants who often go on to take part in further development courses or training. The course takes the form of group activities, and ends with a final challenge or celebration at the end of the course, which is based on the skills and knowledge gained. After completion of the course participants receive three months support related to further training, programmes, volunteer roles, education or employment.

XL Programme

This programme takes the form of a club and is usually run through schools, Pupil Referral Units or Prince's Trust Centres. The aim is to re-engage young people by making learning attractive to them, and for this reason the clubs are informal in nature. Participants are offered a choice of units in five areas, which are:

- Citizenship
- Personal skills, interpersonal skills and team building
- Preparation for employment
- Entrepreneurship and enterprise
- Enrichment through projects

This programme has proved successful since it launched in 1998 and has helped more than 60,000 young people. The clubs currently operate in 600 schools and Prince's Trust Centres throughout the UK. 90% of the young people that take part learn new skills which help them to progress into further education, training or employment.

Leaving Prison Mentoring

Through this scheme former offenders act as supporters to young offenders, inspiring and motivating them to make positive changes to their lives. Supporters visit prisons and give motivational talks to young offenders. They are then paired with a particular youngster who they provide support to in the form of regular meetings during the last six months of their prison sentence as well as additional support once they are released. This additional support entails meeting the young person as they are released from prison and continuing motivational meetings for a further six months post release.

Supporters also act as a positive role model to assist the young person during their transition from prison life into becoming a member of the community. Additionally, they give practical support, for example, helping the young person to access accommodation, benefits or health care.

Enterprise Programme

The Enterprise programme was formerly known as the Business programme and it is designed to help young unemployed people start out in business. Support is both practical and financial and The Prince's Trust has been offering this type of help since 1983. Success rates are high with 56% of businesses now in at least their third year of trading.

Practical support takes the form of mentoring for two years, help with producing a business plan, seminars, self-help kits, advice lines and marketing assistance.

In terms of financial help, participants can access low cost loans of up to £4000 for an individual or £5000 for a partnership. Other financial support is available in the form of start-up grants and test marketing grants.

Leaving Care Mentoring

This is a pilot scheme that works in a similar way to the Leaving Prison Mentoring scheme. The young person in care has a mentor who works as a volunteer. As well as inspiring young people to make positive changes to their lives mentors also offer practical help. For example, they will assist them in accessing health care, housing and benefits when they leave care.

Support lasts for one year and during that time the mentor will meet the young person either once a fortnight or once a month. He will help the young person to set positive goals and achieve them.

Other Help

The Prince's Trust also provides grants in the form of:

Development Awards - These are awards of between £50 and £500 to help young people fund education, training or work.

You can find out more about the work of The Prince's Trust at their website at: www.princes-trust.org.uk.

Who can join?

If you think your child would qualify for one of the programmes detailed in this chapter, please refer to the section below, entitled, 'How to join a Prince's Trust Programme or Course', for further details.

All of The Prince's Trust programmes are aimed at particular groups of young people as mentioned in the preceding section. We have given further details for each of the programmes listed under this section. The programmes are also for specific age groups. Details are as follows:

Team Programme

The qualifying age group is 16-25 and the course is aimed at the long-term unemployed, young offenders, educational underachievers, and those that have been in care.

Fairbridge Programme

This programme is aimed at young people from the ages of 13 to 25 who need help in developing the skills and positive experiences that will help them to re-engage in society.

Get into…

This programme is aimed at unemployed young people from the ages of 16 to 25.

Get Started

Young people aged between 16 and 25 are eligible for this short course. They are also usually from disadvantaged groups, such as young offenders, educational underachievers, those leaving care or long-term unemployed young people.

XL Programme

This programme is for 13 to 19 year olds who are either educational underachievers, at risk of being excluded from school or attending a Pupil Referral Unit.

Leaving Prison Mentoring

This programme is for young people aged between 16 and 30 who want help with settling back into the community and are six months away from the end of their prison sentences.

Supporters are former offenders who have spent time in prison, but have not been in trouble with the law or committed any substance abuse for at least the last two years.

This is a pilot scheme which is currently operating in the South East, the South West and Northern Ireland so it is currently only available in those areas.

Enterprise Programme

Young unemployed people between the ages of 18 and 30 can apply for support through the Enterprise programme. They should be able to demonstrate that they have been unable to raise finance through other means, such as bank loans.

Leaving Care Mentoring

This scheme is aimed at young people leaving care and is currently available in Essex, Slough, Northampton and Pembrokeshire. However, young people leaving care can also obtain booklets from the National Care Advisory Service through The Prince's Trust. These are entitled: 'Know your rights, know your benefits - welfare benefits guide for young people' and 'Employment handbook for young people'. You can obtain these at:

www.princes-trust.org.uk/about_the_trust/what_we_do/programmes/leaving_care_mentoring.aspx using the links towards the bottom of the page under the heading: 'New handbooks created by National Care Advisory Service'.

Benefits

Each programme has its own benefits so we have listed them under the relevant headings, as follows:

Team Programme

- Helps to raise self-esteem and confidence
- Experience of working as part of a team
- Helps to develop a caring attitude towards others
- Participants gain a recognised qualification
- Helps to gain a sense of responsibility
- Participants can discover hidden talents
- Helps to build motivation and plan for the future

Fairbridge Programme

- One to one support and advice
- Participants can tailor the programme to suit their needs
- Develops confidence and self-esteem
- Participants develop self-awareness, motivation and responsibility for their own actions
- Access to ongoing opportunities
- The chance to gain recognised qualifications

Get into …

- Participants gain practical skills and experience relating to a particular employment sector
- Participants take part in interview practice and have help preparing CVs
- The chance to gain a qualification related to the specific employment sector

- Improved employability skills, such as reliability, team work and communication

Get Started

- It builds confidence
- Participants learn new skills
- The chance to access further opportunities for personal development
- Participants feel inspired by taking part in an activity they enjoy
- Opportunities to work as part of a group

XL Programme

- Helps young people to re-engage with learning
- Increases young people's chances of completing compulsory education
- Increases confidence and self-esteem
- Teaches social and behavioural skills
- Improves motivation and increases attendance levels
- Increases young people's chances of employment
- Teaches enterprise skills

Leaving Prison Mentoring

For young offenders the benefits are:

- Being inspired and motivated by someone who has been in a similar situation and managed to turn their life around
- Receiving practical support from their mentor
- Receiving emotional support as they make the transition from prison life back into the community

For supporters who are former offenders the benefits are:

- Developing skills relating to mentoring young people
- Gaining work experience in a voluntary capacity
- Gaining the satisfaction of helping somebody to turn their life around

Enterprise Programme

- Participants receive practical business support and advice
- Participants can apply for a low-interest loan to help start up their businesses
- It helps young people explore the world of self-employment
- Participants acquire valuable information relating to the business world
- Participants get the chance to work in their choice of business

- It can lead to a rewarding and profitable future

Leaving Care Mentoring

For young people leaving care the benefits are:

- Receiving inspiration and motivation from a mentor
- Receiving practical help and advice from a mentor
- Support in setting and achieving goals
- Becoming prepared for a life outside of care

For mentors the benefits are:

- Gaining satisfaction from helping a young person to change their life
- Learning new skills relating to mentoring
- Gaining work experience in a voluntary capacity

Costs

The programmes that are available through The Prince's Trust are usually free of charge to successful applicants.

How to join a Prince's Trust Programme or Course

The Prince's Trust website has an online enquiry form for young people to complete if they are interested in joining one of the programmes. You can find the form at:

www.princes-trust.org.uk/need_help/enquiry_form.aspx.

Becoming Involved as a Parent

There are many ways in which you can support The Prince's Trust. These include volunteer opportunities, support through your company or organization or through making donations. You can find out more about ways to help at: www.princes-trust.org.uk/support_us.aspx.

Chapter 19 - Youth Clubs

Overview

Youth clubs date back to the late 19th Century when most young men finished school at the age of 14 and wanted a place to socialise after work. To cater for the growing number of such clubs the National Association of Boys' Clubs (NABC) was formed in 1925. The NABC evolved over the years, adapting through difficult periods, such as war and recession. During the 80s and 90s it ran volunteer schemes for the unemployed, teaching them skills to help them secure future employment.

Clubs for Young People

(www.clubsforyoungpeople.org.uk)

Eventually the NABC changed its focus to recognise the fact that youth clubs were also directed at females. Several name changes followed and the present name of 'Clubs for Young People' has been used since 2005.

Most youth clubs in the UK operate on an informal basis so activities vary with some having a slant towards a particular theme, such as religious guidance. Others offer support to young people regarding employment, and other personal and social issues, as well as offering a place to socialise with peers. Although activities vary according to the particular club's interests and finances, typical pastimes include table tennis, snooker, pool, computer games, sports, music and board games.

Youth clubs are usually operated by community groups, schools, churches and charities. They meet at specific times, usually once or twice a week, in churches, schools, community centres or other local authority buildings.

There is currently no requirement for youth clubs to belong to a particular association or organization. However, Clubs for Young People is trying to support them and give them a more formalised structure. It currently helps more than 3,500 youth clubs and defines itself as, 'The leading charity for youth clubs and community projects'. The organization's website defines it as follows:

'Clubs for Young People helps young people to achieve their potential through social and personal development opportunities. We provide support to our network of members, as well as deliver a national programme of initiatives.'

There are also regional groups that support their member youth clubs, such as:

The Boys and Girls Clubs of Greater Manchester (www.bgcgm.org.uk) - This organization targets young people from the ages of 9 to 22, and works with member clubs to provide support and training.

In 2009 Clubs for Young People developed a blueprint, which is intended to shape the future of youth clubs in the UK giving them a more structured, co-ordinated and defined role. Additionally, clubs will be provided with training, support and monitoring. Because of the influence of Clubs for Young People we could see a shift in the focus of youth clubs, with more emphasis placed on the personal development of young people whilst still maintaining the social aspect.

Groups that are focused on developing young people already exist, such as UK Youth, and The Prince's Trust, which is featured in Chapter 18. UK Youth is a membership organization for other groups involved with youths in the UK rather than an association that deals direct with young people and their parents; therefore it is not featured in this book. Other groups covered in this book help young people to achieve their potential but they are geared towards a specific sector e.g. the armed forces or the emergency services.

Who can join?

Youth clubs are generally aimed at teenagers but age ranges differ from club to club with some starting from as young as nine and others catering for ages up to early twenties. It is best to enquire with the specific club to find out what the age requirements are. Youth clubs may have other stipulations for membership, for example, some clubs still operate for boys only or girls only.

Benefits

The benefits derived from attending a youth club will vary depending on the aims of the particular club and its activities, but in general terms these are likely to include:

- The chance to socialise and make new friends
- An increase in confidence and self-esteem
- An opportunity to try new activities and pastimes
- Keeping young people occupied and out of mischief
- A chance to be physically active and take part in team activities rather than spending time alone in front of the TV or computer

Additionally, some clubs teach life skills in a supportive environment and some offer the chance to become involved in worthwhile projects that benefit the community.

Costs

Costs vary but as youth clubs tend to be run as charities the entrance fees are usually very low. Again, it is best to check with specific youth clubs.

How to Find a Youth Club

Clubs for Young People is a good starting point as it has more than 3500 affiliated youth clubs. The contact page of the website is:

www.clubsforyoungpeople.org.uk/page.asp?section=44&sectionTitle=Contact+us.

If you are in the Greater Manchester region, you could get in touch with BGCGM to find out about clubs in your area. Their email address is: admin@bgcgm.org.uk and the telephone number is: 0161 477 7765.

Other areas may have an umbrella organization that will have member youth clubs. You may find an organization in your area by typing the name of your area and 'youth clubs' in an Internet search engine.

For all other regions, if you cannot find a youth club through Clubs for Young People, you could try the following sources of information: your local library, schools in your area, your local authority or an Internet search engine. Often you can find out about youth clubs through word of mouth amongst your children's peer group.

Becoming Involved as a Parent

Clubs for Young People welcomes volunteers to help with its work and it also has a limited number of paid positions through its network of more than 40 organizations in various areas of the country.

You can find out more about volunteer work with 'Clubs for Young People' at:

www.clubsforyoungpeople.org.uk/page.asp?section =85&sectionTitle=Volunteers. You may also find opportunities to help out at your local youth club by enquiring with the staff there.

Chapter 20 - The Great Outdoors

Overview

For children the great outdoors can present a whole world of adventure and excitement. There are many critics nowadays who say that children don't play out as much as they should. This is understandable though, when parents have concerns about the dangers posed, as well as a lack of time to spend supervising their children in outdoor activities. However, there are many opportunities offered by organizations at little or no cost. These can give children the chance to take part in a wide range of outdoor activities including: rambling, orienteering, abseiling and potholing as well as many more.

The previous chapters of this book cover many organizations that offer outdoor ventures as part of their activities. These include, for example, the Boys' and Girls' Brigades, The Scout Association, Girl Guides, the Duke of Edinburgh's Award and the various organizations connected to the Armed Forces. In addition to these there are a number of other organizations that offer outdoor activities and holiday camps. We have given details of some of the larger, national ones below, but you may find others situated locally. The Young Explorers' Trust could help with this and we have given details in our later section headed 'How to Find a Group'.

The Ramblers (www.ramblers.org.uk)

The Ramblers dates back to the nineteenth Century and is a charitable organization, which was set up with the aim of keeping public footpaths open to enable people to enjoy the countryside. There are now more than 500 walking groups throughout the UK, which not only organize local walks, but are also involved in campaigning to preserve the walking environment. The Ramblers is the biggest walking charity in Britain and has approximately 120,000 members.

Walks are graded according to difficulty and many walks are also themed. There is a regular programme of walks and events throughout the year in various parts of the UK, and the association promotes walking in the city as well as in the countryside.

Young Archaeologists' Club (www.yac-uk.org)

The Young Archaeologist's Club (YAC) is run by the Council for British Archaeology, which is an educational charity, and it has been running for almost 40 years. It is the only national UK club dedicated to children up to the age of 17 who are interested in archaeology.

Children who are members of YAC UK receive: a membership card, badge and certificate, a welcome letter, a pass booklet and a quarterly magazine. The pass book, together with the membership card, gives discounts to archaeological sites across the UK, of which there are more than 184 working in partnership with YAC. The website has a map of these sites at: www.yac-uk.org/yacpass/map, which is interactive so if you click on a specific site you can see details of current offers. Members are also informed of archaeology related events that take place across the UK.

In addition, YAC runs individual branches around the UK, which children can join. There are about 70 branches altogether, but you will sometimes have to put your child's name on a waiting list as demand for places is high. Even membership of YAC UK does not guarantee that your child will automatically get a place at a branch. Branches usually meet once a month and are run by adult volunteers who are all CRB checked and are vetted for safety by the YAC approvals panel.

The Outward Bound Trust

(www.outwardbound.org.uk)

The Outward Bound Trust is an educational charity which was established over 70 years ago. Its original purpose was as a survival school for merchant seamen who might become shipwrecked and have to endure harsh conditions. After the war the value of the Outward Bound Trust was recognised in helping young people to develop

170

valuable life skills and enabling them to become more independent and self-aware. Survival skills are taught outdoors in a natural environment by a team of qualified instructors. The Outward Bound Trust also has high standards of safety and has public liability insurance.

Rather than a regular club the Outward Bound Trust runs courses for either eight days or 22 days duration. These are mentally and physically demanding and are best for young people who already have a good level of fitness. The courses usually run from a Saturday to a Saturday during school holidays and are described as 'adventures'.

There are a number of types of adventures aimed at different age groups and these are held at various locations. Typical activities include: learning to build a camp fire, hill walking, learning to build a raft, rock climbing and kayaking. You can find out more about the different courses, including the dates and locations where they are held at: www.outwardbound.org.uk/individual-participants/adventures-a-expeditions.html.

PGL Adventure Holidays and Summer Camps

(www.pgl.co.uk/pglweb)

PGL is a privately run company, but it has been established for over 50 years and places a high emphasis on safety and security. As well as camps for kids, which are known as Adventure Holidays, the company also offers Family Activity Holidays, School Trips and Courses, and Group Residentials. The latter are for organizations such as the Brownies, Scouts and youth clubs. There are 13 adventure centres in the UK, three in France and two in Austria.

In terms of the Adventure Holidays offered to individual children, the types of activities depend on the age group, but they are extensive. The holidays are themed, with each given a title so, for example, there are holidays called, 'Martial Arts', 'Climbing Adventure', 'Cook's Academy', 'Film Making' and many more. As suggested by the titles, not all of the activities take place outdoors; it all depends on the holiday that your child or children choose.

For children that are looking for all round adventure, there is an 'Introductory Adventure', which is of two or three days duration and gives children a taste of what the holidays have to offer. The most popular holiday is the 'Multi Activity' holiday, which lasts for six days and is open to children aged from 7 to 16 at various locations throughout the UK. This holiday includes more than 50 activities, such as motorcycling, abseiling, kayaking and fencing. Not all holidays are available at all centres so you may decide to base your choice on location. You can find more details of all the Adventure Holidays at:

www.pgl.co.uk/pglweb/individuals/holidaylist.

KG Adventure

(http://adventurecamps.kgadventure.com)

KG specialises in Adventure Camps for children aged from 6 to 16. It is part of the wider Klub Group Ltd, which has a worldwide reach. KG operates a code of practice and places emphasis on the care and safety of children who attend camps. This means that the company takes account of any medical conditions, special needs or dietary requirements for children attending camps and has qualified first-aiders on hand.

The company offers either residential camps or day camps in England, which all take place during school holidays. Residential camps usually run for seven days from either Saturday to Saturday or Sunday to Sunday. However, there is an option to have a short residential stay of three days and two nights. Locations are restricted though for short stay camps.

Activities take place indoors or outdoors and children have a choice of focusing on either adventure, sports or creativity. Children will have a weekly programme, which includes four core activities a day. There are also fun activities in the evenings, such as discos, talent shows, table tennis and parachute games.

KG also offers two European camps. The first is a skiing and snowboarding holiday for teenagers in the Swiss Alps. The second European camp is a thirteen night holiday in Spain. As well as many activities, the Spanish camp also includes language lessons.

Wildlife Trusts and Nature Reserves

(www.wildlifetrusts.org/who-we-are)

We have given details of The Wildlife Trusts and Nature Reserves in chapter 13 - Animals and Pets. The junior section of The Wildlife Trusts is called Wildlife Watch, which has local groups throughout the UK. The groups hold regular meetings where children take place in various interesting activities relating to wildlife and the environment. Full details of age requirements, costs etc can be found in chapter 13.

Who can join?

Membership of the above groups is usually restricted to certain age groups so we have given details of these where appropriate, as follows:

The Rambler's Association - There are many walks which are specifically designed for people with children, but you are responsible for supervision of your children during these walks. You can find more information about organized walks suitable for children at:

www.ramblers.org.uk/areas_groups/areas_and_grou ps.

Older children aged from 15-17 can attend walks alone but they have to have consent from their parents. You can apply for a consent card through the website by going to the page relating to walks for people with children per the above link. On this page of the website there is a section headed, 'Children and young people', which has a link to a PDF document that gives you all the details you need.

Young Archaeologists' Club - Membership of YAC UK is open to children up to the age of 17. YAC Branches are for children from the ages of 8 to 17.

The Outward Bound Trust - Children and young people from the ages of 11 to 24 can take part in adventure camps as Individual Participants, but the Trust also has programmes and courses for schools and colleges and for corporate development.

PGL Adventure Holidays and Summer Camps - PGL has adventure holidays to suit children from the ages of 7 to 17, with different types of holidays being offered to specific age groups. The age groups are: 7 - 10, 10 - 13 and 13 - 16 for UK holidays, and 9 - 13 and 13 - 17 for holidays overseas. The website has full details of holidays for each age group.

KG Adventure - Holidays are for children from 6 to 16, but different camps cater to different age groups within this age range. You can find out more at: http://adventurecamps.kgadventure.com/uk-camps, which has links to further information including a brochure that you can download from the website.

Benefits

The mere act of spending time outdoors will be of benefit to your children as they will experience a sense of freedom and excitement as well as being able to breathe in fresh air. Other benefits will depend on the type of activities, but in general these will include:

- A chance for children to keep fit and healthy whilst enjoying themselves
- Opportunities to learn valuable life skills
- Improved social skills through interacting with other children and young people
- An increase in self-esteem and self-awareness through completion of outdoor challenges
- Children learn to appreciate their natural environment

- A chance for children to try activities that they may not normally experience
- A break for parents whilst their children are at camp

Costs

Some outdoor activities are completely free. For example, you could take your children for regular walks in the countryside and it will not cost you a thing. Also, some of the organizations named above do not necessarily charge for individual membership, for example, the Young Explorer's Trust, which is really more of an umbrella organization that other bodies are connected to. However, other groups will charge, therefore, where appropriate, we have listed costs under each of these groups or organizations, as follows:

The Rambler's Association - Membership is free for children under the age of 16. However, children up to the age of 14 must be accompanied by an adult on walks and children aged 15 to 17 need a consent card, which is covered in our 'Who can join?' section above.

The Association will allow non-members to join national festival walks and some events. Regular walks are usually aimed at members but you can try out a couple of walks free of charge prior to joining.

<u>Young Archaeologists' Club</u> - Membership of YAC UK costs £15 per annum for children up to 17. There is also a membership for multiple children of up to five in the same family and this costs £21 per annum.

Branch charges vary; some don't charge at all, some charge for each meeting you attend and others make an annual charge. You can find out how much your nearest branch charges for attendance by contacting the Branch leader. To find his details, visit the branch finder at: <u>www.yac-uk.org/branches/map</u>, and click on the branch of your choice.

<u>The Outward Bound Trust</u> - Prices start at £399 fully inclusive for an eight day adventure. However, as the Outward Bound Trust is a charity it is possible to get financial assistance. This takes the form of up to 50% course funding from the Trust's Bursary scheme. You can find out more about financial assistance at:

<u>www.outwardbound.org.uk/individual-participants/financial-assistance.html</u>.

<u>PGL Adventure Holidays and Summer Camps</u> - Although this is a privately run group they do have relatively inexpensive options for summer camps, which give children a short taster experience. They offer a two days, one night introductory adventure holiday for £99, or three days, two nights for £135. For lengthier holidays prices vary depending on the

duration and choice of activities. You can find more details of the different options at:

www.pgl.co.uk/PglWeb/individuals. NB PGL also runs special offers, which you can find out about on the website.

KG Adventure - Day camps are the cheapest option with prices starting from £29 per day or £120 for Monday to Friday. Short stays of three days and two nights cost £125, and seven day stays cost from £365 per week depending on the time of year.

How to Find a Group

Some of the above organizations have various branches in different regions, whereas for others, particularly summer camps, you would have to travel. We have therefore given details of how to find further information for each of these bodies, where appropriate:

The Rambler's Association - The Rambler's Association website has a sophisticated search facility with different search options. The advanced search enables you to find walks in your area based on dates, level of difficulty, theme, distance and facilities, such as whether the walk is suitable for buggies and wheelchairs. You can access the search facility at:

www.ramblers.org.uk/areas_groups/groupswalksfinder.htm.

<u>Young Archaeologists' Club</u> - Membership of YAC UK is a magazine based subscription, which you can find out about on the website at: <u>www.yac-uk.org/about</u>. Membership of a branch is separate and you can find your nearest branch on YAC's interactive map at: <u>www.yac-uk.org/branches/map</u>.

<u>The Outward Bound Trust</u> - Adventures take place at three different locations depending on the type of adventure. The three locations are: Loch Eil in the Highlands of Scotland, Aberdovey in Snowdonia, Wales, and Ullswater in the Lake District. The specific location will be detailed in the information relating to that particular adventure on the Adventures and Expeditions page of the website, which is: <u>www.outwardbound.org.uk/individual-participants/adventures-a-expeditions.html</u>.

You can also try the <u>Young Explorers' Trust</u> website at: <u>www.theyet.org</u>. This is a body that other groups involved in expeditions for young people become members of, rather than children themselves directly becoming members. However, they have a number of approved bodies shown on a dedicated web page at:

<u>www.theyet.org/approved_expeditions.php</u>,

so children and parents can look here for details of the groups.

<u>PGL Adventure Holidays and Summer Camps</u> - You can find details of PGL's centres at:

www.pgl.co.uk/PglWeb/individuals/locations. Bear in mind that not all of the centres offer every type of holiday, but the website does give details of where each type of holiday takes place.

<u>KG Adventure</u> - You can find details of KG centres at:

http://adventurecamps.kgadventure.com/uk-camps/directions.

This web page shows the location of each particular camp with further details on the types of activities held at that camp.

<u>Becoming Involved as a Parent</u>

There are many ways in which parents can become involved, ranging from organizing your own outdoor activities for your children, to joining one of the above groups. Opportunities open to parents are as follows:

<u>The Rambler's Association </u>- There are a number of membership options for adults, some of which are annual and some of which provide membership for life. Individual annual membership costs £19.50 for concessionary and £31.00 for non-concessionary, but there are also joint memberships for two adults, which work out cheaper per person.

Apart from being able to take part in organized walks, members also receive: a free magazine, discounts at a recommended outdoor retailer, access to maps which you can borrow for a small fee, and offers on walking holidays.

Young Archaeologists' Club - Adults from the age of 17 can become members of YAC UK at a cost of £15 a year. This entitles them to receive the quarterly Young Archaeologist magazine, a booklet with special offers, the Festival of British Archaeology booklet once a year, details of events, and information on becoming a volunteer. You can also find out about becoming a branch volunteer through the website at:

www.yac-uk.org/faq/branchvolunteer.

The Outward Bound Trust - The courses themselves are aimed at children and young people so you would not be able to attend a course with your children. However, if you are interested in getting involved with the Outward Bound Trust there are two ways that you can do so. The first is by making a donation, as the Outward Bound Trust is a charity. You can find out more at:

www.outwardbound.org.uk/support-the-trust.html.

The second way in which you can get involved is by having a career with the Outward Bound Trust, or working as a local volunteer, helping to raise funds for the Trust. Please bear in mind that to have a career with the Outward Bound Trust you would need outdoor qualifications, but this does not apply with the type of volunteer work that we have described. You can find out more about these opportunities at:

www.outwardbound.org.uk/careers.html.

PGL Adventure Holidays and Summer Camps - If you prefer to spend holidays with your children rather than letting them go alone, PGL also have Family Activity Holidays. There are seven different holidays to choose from at various locations and you can expect to be kept very busy throughout your holiday. You can find out more at:

www.pgl.co.uk/PGLWeb/Families/.

Chapter 21 - Academic Classes

Overview

There could be various reasons for enrolling your children in academic classes or clubs in addition to the classes already studied at school. This could be, for example, because your children find certain subjects challenging and need extra support. Alternatively they may want to study a subject that is not available in school or has limited availability on the school curriculum. You may also find that your child has an avid interest in a particular subject (such as computing or arts and crafts), and wants to increase his/her knowledge in that area. NB These academic classes are in addition to the clubs run by local authorities that sometimes use school facilities, which were discussed in chapter 13. Provision for additional academic classes is available both in the private and public sectors, as follows:

Schools

You may find that your child's school offers additional non-compulsory lessons outside of school hours. These lessons may offer opportunities that are not covered by the national curriculum, for example, the chance to study a language at a younger age. Therefore, school is a good starting point if you want your child to attend extra classes especially as these are usually offered free of charge.

Colleges

Secondly, local colleges sometimes offer classes for school children, but provision varies from region to region. We will take Tameside College in Greater Manchester as an example. As well as having a crèche for younger children, which takes care of children whilst their parents are studying, the college also offers classes for teenagers from the ages of 14 to 16. The college works in partnership with local schools to provide opportunities for pupils to gain recognised qualifications, such as City and Guilds and OCR certificates. Studies can be combined with work experience to prepare pupils for future careers.

The college also offers a number of part-time courses, which can be attended either on day release from school or one evening a week after school. These classes are vocational in nature and therefore give children the chance to study subjects that they wouldn't otherwise study through school. Additionally, the classes give children a taste of college life and can help to set them on a particular career pathway. However, for day release courses, pupils will probably not be able to study as many GCSEs because one or two days a week will be devoted to their college course.

Subjects currently on offer through Tameside College are: Motor Vehicle, Bakery, Construction, Engineering, Sport, Hairdressing, Child Care, Travel and Tourism, Catering, IT, Dance, Art and Design, Media, Hospitality, Drama and Beauty Therapy. Details of all Tameside College courses for 14 to 16 year olds are available at:

www.tameside.ac.uk/Pages/14-16_School_Pupils/Default.aspx.

The Private Sector

Many individual teachers offer extra tuition, which they will either provide at their designated premises or sometimes they will attend your home. If you are going to apply to a private tutor make sure that the person is a qualified teacher and has met the appropriate requirements in terms of CRB checks.

Apart from individuals in the private sector there is a growing trend for groups to offer extra private tuition in many areas of the UK. Again, you should ensure that appropriate checks have been carried out and that the group meets health and safety requirements. Here are details of two of the larger groups, but you may also find others that cover specific regions of the UK:

Kumon

(www.kumon.co.uk) - Kumon is a supplementary education provider offering maths and English

Programmes to children of all ages and abilities. The Kumon Method was developed in Japan in 1954 by Toru Kumon. The founder was a high school mathematics teacher who decided to help his son to improve his maths results. He instructed his son using a series of worksheets and his method was so successful that he began to help other children in the neighbourhood. The Kumon Institute of Education was established in 1958 in Japan and was so successful that many other centres soon opened throughout Japan, eventually spreading overseas.

The Kumon Institute launched its Maths Programme in 1983 in the UK and its English Programme in 1997. There are now over 630 Kumon centres in the UK, which operate as franchises.

Through the Kumon Method children begin at a level that suits them and progress through the programmes at their own pace. The requirements for each level are tailored to each individual child, and the levels gradually become more advanced.

Extra Tuition Centre (www.extratuition.com) - The Extra Tuition Centre (ETC) started in Kent over 40 years ago, but it now has branches based in more than 20 locations throughout the UK. Although the majority of branches are situated in the south of the country, new centres are continually being opened.

They teach two subjects, which are English and maths, but also teach verbal and non verbal reasoning for the 11 plus exams. Their approach covers five stages. The first stage is to assess the child's needs; this enables the tutors to go on to develop a personalised learning plan (stage 2). The third stage is for continual self assessment, and the centres issue twice yearly reports (stage 4). The final stage of their approach culminates in each child being able to reach their full potential.

The group works with schools and Local Education Authorities and has a range of courses developed to help children pass their SATs tests, 11 plus exams and GCSEs. Teachers and classroom assistants are trained in the ETC method, which focuses on personalised learning plans to suit children of varying abilities.

Who can join?

Academic classes and clubs are available for all children but availability in both the public and private sectors will depend on the age group of your child or children as well as other factors. For instance, schools that provide extra classes will tailor these for a particular age group. Likewise, college classes will suit certain ages, such as the courses at Tameside College that we referred to above, which are specifically for 14 to 16 year olds.

Additionally, many colleges work in partnership with schools, so applications for vocational college courses will often have to be made through your child's school. Generally, where extra classes are offered by your children's school these will usually only apply to pupils that attend that school.

With regard to private tuition, many tutors will specialise in specific subjects and certain stages of the national curriculum so it is best to check with them. Also, provision in the private sector will be subject to fees, which vary from tutor to tutor and from tuition group to tuition group. You can find further details relating to fees in our 'Costs' section. Regarding the two private tuition groups that we mentioned above, details are as follows:

Kumon - Children of any age or ability can join Kumon subject to there being a Kumon Centre within commuting distance of your home and to paying the requisite fees. You can find out more about enrolment at: www.kumon.co.uk/how-to-enrol.

Extra Tuition Centre - The ETC caters for children from the ages of 6 to 16 including those with special needs. Attendance is at one of the 20+ centres throughout the UK, and is subject to payment of the requisite fees. Some work is carried out online and children attend for varying periods from a couple of weeks to long-term. You can contact the ETC for more information at:

www.extratuition.com/contactus.html, and can find out more about locations and fees in the sections below.

Benefits

There can be many benefits of attending academic clubs and classes for children. However, it is also important to bear in mind that children can feel overburdened if they are already spending a great deal of time on their studies. Benefits include:

- The chance to study different topics than those studied at school
- An opportunity to gain vocational qualifications
- A chance for children to experience a more practical approach by combining studies with work experience
- Enhanced career prospects through vocational courses
- Help for children who may find certain subjects challenging
- A chance for children to meet new people often with similar career aspirations
- A taste of college life through college classes

- An opportunity for children to study at their own pace
- Increased self-esteem through achieving higher marks at school
- A chance for children to try different study approaches that may suit them better than the methods used in mainstream schools
- Helping children to catch up with their schoolwork following holidays or illness

Costs

The public sector is the lowest cost option with classes often free or charged at a nominal amount. In the case of college classes that are provided in partnership with schools, you may find that your child's school will fund the cost of the course, as is the case with the Tameside College scheme.

Private Tuition - You can get an idea of tutoring costs at the following link:

www.hometutorsdirectory.co.uk/TutorGuide.html# Tutoringcosts. Bear in mind that fees will be higher in the South of the country and that individual lessons will be more expensive than group lessons.

Kumon - Study costs vary for each Kumon centre to reflect the centre's running costs. However, each centre will charge a registration fee and a monthly fee per subject for each child.

Extra Tuition Centre - Costs depend on a number of factors, such as the age group, subjects and duration, but the following are a typical example of the level of charges you can expect:

Kent location - lessons for all age groups are charged at £15 per hour.

Manchester location - a three day summer revision course for 11+ students is offered at a total cost of £120.00.

How to Find a Group

A good starting point is to enquire through your child's school. If they do not offer extra tuition then you can either try your local authority for details of local colleges that offer extra tuition for children, or approach the colleges direct. It is a good idea to look at the college websites as these provide a host of information, and reception staff at the colleges may not always be aware of all that is on offer.

Private Tuition - People offering private tuition will usually advertise in telephone directories, the local press and through the Internet. Sometimes you might find a tutor through recommendations.

There are two useful websites, which give details relating to private tutors. The first of these is the Home Tutors Directory at:

www.hometutorsdirectory.co.uk. This website is a useful resource. It has a guide to employing a tutor, giving advice on the questions to ask and what to look out for, and it enables you to search for a tutor according to subject and UK region.

The second useful website is:

www.kidsguide.co.uk. Once you've entered this website, select your region, then select 'extra tuition' under the heading 'Clubs and Classes'. This is a more generalised site than the Home Tutors Directory, so although it gives a list of people and organizations providing extra tuition in your area with links to their websites, it doesn't give advice related specifically to finding a private tutor.

Kumon - The Kumon website has an interactive map, which enables you to find details of the centre nearest to your home. You can access it at:

www.kumon.co.uk/map.

Extra Tuition Centre - The website has details of all the ETC centres at:

www.extratuition.com/learning_centres.html.

Becoming Involved as a Parent

Whether you wish to involve your child in extra academic classes or clubs is down to you and the wishes of your child. Many children benefit from extra tuition but others feel overburdened if they have too much academic work to get through.

Another factor regarding extra tuition is whether you think your child will benefit from following a more vocational route. In year nine of Secondary School children select their subjects from various options. Many schools will suggest a route of study for years 10 and 11 based on your child's career aspirations and abilities. Your child's school may also ask you to visit the school and speak to a teacher regarding your child's subject choices. If your child's school doesn't offer this opportunity and you have concerns or wish to find out more about study options, you should arrange to visit the school and speak to a member of staff.

The Kumon group described above offers franchise opportunities for those who wish to become involved in education. You can find out more about becoming a Kumon franchisee at:

www.kumon.co.uk/franchise. Kumon also has a number of offices around the country which support the work of its centres. There are career opportunities in these offices in fields such as IT, finance, marketing, communications and human resources. You can find out more at:

www.kumon.co.uk/careers.

The Extra Tuition Centre also has career opportunities for adults; roles include teachers, teaching assistants, assessors and learning support assistants. You can find out more at:

www.extratuition.com/job-vacancies.html.

Chapter 22 - Groups for Gifted Children

Overview

The UK Government describes gifted children as those "with an ability to develop to a level significantly ahead of their year group (or with the potential to develop those abilities)". The term 'gifted' usually applies to academic abilities. Talented children, on the other hand, excel in more practical areas, such as sports, music and drama. Many schools recognize gifted and talented students and provide extra challenges to help them achieve their full potential. Some schools have a co-ordinator for gifted and talented education and some local authorities have a gifted and talented lead.

If you feel that your child is gifted but is not receiving any additional support through school you should discuss it with either your child's school, or with your local authority gifted and talented lead, if it has one. Alternatively, you can receive support through the National Association for Gifted Children, which we will discuss below.

It is a common misconception that gifted children do not need any extra help and support, because they don't usually struggle with their schoolwork. Being gifted presents its own challenges and these children need support to help them channel their giftedness so that they can achieve their full potential. The National Association for Gifted Children prefers to use the term 'High Learning Potential' rather than 'gifted' because there is a lot of stigma and high expectations attached to the word 'gifted'.

Gifted children have what is known as asynchronous development. This means that they develop intellectually at a much faster rate than they develop emotionally, socially and physically. Therefore, they tend to have high energy levels and a vivid imagination, and are more sensitive and emotional than many other children. Because they are quite intense, they can often be viewed by others as weird or odd. This can affect self-esteem.

In addition, time in the classroom can pass very slowly and seem boring for gifted children if they are not met with sufficient challenges. When they race ahead and constantly ask for more work they can be viewed by their peers as show-offs or attention seekers. For this reason they can also become the victims of bullying. Some gifted children can display challenging behaviour as a result of their frustration.

Apart from the emotional perspective, gifted children approach study in a different way and this doesn't always work to their advantage. Because they think in such a complex and abstract way they often skip instructions as they are impatient to jump to the next task. This can sometimes result in poor test results. Again this can affect their self-esteem, especially since such high expectations are often placed on them. Boredom can also affect their grades at school. Gifted children therefore benefit from being consistently challenged academically and they work well when placed with other students who have similar abilities.

It can be demanding being a parent of a gifted child as they need to be stimulated constantly and this can be exhausting at times. There are further difficulties for children who have Dual or Multiple Exceptionality. This means that as well as being gifted they have special educational needs, such as dyslexia, dyspraxia or ADHD. Many gifted children have Dual or Multiple Exceptionality so they need added support. As a parent you can help to provide some of the support that your child needs and the NAGC website at www.nagcbritain.org.uk is full of useful tips and advice.

The National Association for Gifted Children (NAGC)

The National Association for Gifted Children (NAGC) has been supporting gifted children for over 40 years not only with their learning, but emotionally and socially too. Additionally, it offers support and guidance to parents of gifted children, as well as advising teaching professionals. Support is given through information and advice, training, and activities for gifted children and their families. The NAGC operates as a charity as well as a membership organization, and therefore relies on donations and membership subscriptions.

Members can access the monthly Explorer Clubs for gifted children and their families, which are based at various locations in the UK. These provide enrichment activities for gifted children and enable them to meet other children with similar abilities. By becoming members of the NAGC parents can have two telephone consultations a year with a qualified Education Consultant, can share ideas and concerns with other parents via the Parent's Forum on NAGC's website and can access fact sheets and publications through the website.

Who can join?

This section will relate to membership of the NAGC since that is the organization that provides help and support for gifted children. Membership of the NAGC is open to the following groups:

Families - where at least one gifted child is a family member. If your child has not been identified as gifted through his school but you believe that he may be, you can find more information on identifying High Learning Potential through the NAGC website at:

www.nagcbritain.org.uk/parents.php?webid=251.

Individuals - This type of membership includes teachers, head teachers, health visitors, educational psychologists, youth workers and anybody else with a personal interest in issues related to gifted and talented children.

There are also other types of membership available, such as, 'Friends of NAGC', for people who may no longer need the help of the NAGC but still want to give some support for the work that it does. 'Schools', is another type of membership, for schools and other educational organizations. Reduced membership costs are available for students and those in receipt of various benefits. Further information is available on the NAGC website at:

www.nagcbritain.org.uk/membership.php and in our section below headed 'costs'.

Benefits

As the groups for gifted children are run by the NAGC, for this section we will focus on the benefits of NAGC membership. These are as follows:

- Children feel more comfortable socialising with children of similar abilities
- Children are challenged through enrichment activities

- Children experience increased self-esteem as they feel understood and their needs are being met
- Parents can access professional advice through the telephone consultations with an Education Consultant
- Parents receive support via the Parent's Forum
- Families of gifted children have opportunities to meet other families through the extra events that the NAGC hosts, such as family weekends
- Through this support gifted children are often able to reach their full potential

Costs

Membership of the NAGC offers a whole host of benefits in addition to those already mentioned above. You can find out more at:

www.nagcbritain.org.uk/new_parents_main.php?contentid=241&webid=235. Membership fees are currently as follows:

Family Membership - £42 per annum or £82.80 for three years.

Individual Membership (as defined above) - £36 per annum.

International Membership (for those outside England who have an interest in the NAGC) - £30 per annum.

Friends of NAGC (as defined above) - £15 per annum.

Schools - The costs depend on the category of membership and the type of organization, with prices varying from £100 per annum for a standard or gold primary school membership to £150 per annum for a standard or gold secondary school membership. Three yearly memberships are also available for schools and the price for local authority memberships is available on application.

Students (for full-time students over the age of 18) - £18 per annum.

Concessionary (for people on various benefits and families with foster children) - £18 per annum.

How to Find a Group

Explorers Clubs meet at local branches which are currently based in: Liverpool, Greater Manchester, Cheshire, Hertfordshire, Surrey, Milton Keynes, Northampton, Ipswich, Kent and the West of England. The NAGC are looking for people who want to get involved in setting up more local branches and you can find out more by contacting them by email at:

amazingchildren@nagcbritain.org.uk

or by telephoning: 01908 646433.

Apart from Explorers Club meetings, the NAGC has a regular programme of events. You can find out more about events in your area at:

www.nagcbritain.org.uk/events.aspx.

Becoming Involved as a Parent

A big advantage of family membership of NAGC is that support is also available for parents of gifted children. Through family membership the NAGC helps parents of gifted children in the following ways:

-   Two detailed telephone consultations a year with an Education Consultant and the opportunity to buy a report based on the consultation
-   Access to a telephone advice line
-   Regular newsletters for parents
-   Access to factsheets and other publications
-   Access to a parent's forum via the NAGC website
-   Family activity days, parents' workshops and parents' discussion groups

You can also become more involved by working as a volunteer for the NAGC or by setting up a local group as mentioned in the previous section. You can find out more about volunteering at:

www.nagcbritain.org.uk/volunteers.php.

Chapter 23 - Clubs for Children with Special Needs

Overview

The term 'special needs' covers a wide range of circumstances and situations. For example, this could refer to: disabled children, children with learning disabilities, children who are victims of domestic abuse, children from families with mental illness, young carers and children from poor families.

As this topic covers such a wide spectrum it is beyond the scope of this book to detail every organization in the UK that has clubs for children with special needs. Instead this book acts as a starting point, giving you information to help you find a club that may be suitable for your child's needs. In terms of generalised provision, a primary support organization is 'Action for Children'.

Action for Children (www.actionforchildren.org.uk) is a leading UK organization, which offers advice and support for children with various difficulties, and their families. As part of its support it has a range of facilities and schemes at its Children's Centres, such as child care for children from the ages of 3 to 14, and parent and toddler groups.

It runs more than 120 Children's Centres in the UK, which offer specialist support to children with disabilities, and also helps children (and their families) in the following groups:

- Children who are having problems at school
- Abused or neglected children
- Children who are carers
- Children of separated or divorced parents
- Children from families who risk losing their homes as a result of anti-social behaviour
- Children going through the transition of settling back at home
- Children from families that are at risk of separation

One of the valuable ways in which Action for Children supports disabled children and their families is through short breaks. The organization has been providing short breaks for more than 20 years and is used to supporting families with complex needs. Not only does this help disabled children to enjoy new experiences and have fun, but it also gives the family a break, removing some of the stress involved in day to day care.

Family Action is another organization giving support to disadvantaged families, and it also provides services within Children's Centres. You can find out more about Family Action at: www.family-action.org.uk.

Other Organizations

There are many other organizations that cater for children with various special needs. Some organizations support only children (and adults) with a particular condition, such as Mencap, which supports people with learning disabilities.

However, you will find mainstream organizations that also help children with special needs. In fact, many of the organizations mentioned in this book provide clubs and activities for children with special needs as well as mainstream children. For example, the Princes' Trust, which we discussed in chapter 18 of this book, has many programmes to help disadvantaged young people from the ages of 13 upwards.

Other organizations that you may not necessarily associate with special needs nevertheless have special provisions, such as the Rambler's Association (www.ramblers.org.uk), which aims to make walking accessible to as wide a range of people as possible.

You will also often find support through local authorities. For instance, the Tameside Borough Council's holiday scheme also includes classes for children with disabilities. You can find details of how to access the various clubs, centres and support networks for children with special needs in the section of this chapter headed 'How to Find a Group'.

Who can join?

Different clubs and organizations will have different membership criteria, which will depend on your child's type of special needs. Therefore, it is best to enquire with specific clubs that you feel meet your child's requirements.

Benefits

If your child has special needs he will derive many benefits from attending a club that caters to his particular circumstances. These benefits will vary depending on the particular club, but generally some of the likely benefits are:

- A welcome break for children who are in stressful situations
- Children are nurtured in an environment where their needs are understood
- Targeted help can enable children to develop skills and talents that may have otherwise been undiscovered
- Children can relate to others in similar circumstances
- Children gain confidence and self-esteem through others understanding their situations
- Children and families can often access further sources of help and support through these clubs

- Children can talk through their problems with someone outside the family
- Children feel less isolated and able to ask for support and advice

Costs

As most of these clubs and groups are run as charities, costs are likely to be very low and in some cases they may be free of charge. However, actual costs will vary depending on the particular club or organization.

How to Find a Group

If your child has a particular condition you may have already found a support group that has a children's club. Aside from the various organizations already covered in this book, which may have special needs provision; the following ideas should be useful in helping you to find a group or club:

1) You can find an interactive map of Children's Centres run by Action for Children at:

www.actionforchildren.org.uk/our-services.

2) Have a look at your local authority's website to see if they run any services for people (and in particular children) with special needs.

3) Nasen is the National Association for Special Educational Needs so its focus is more on

education, but it has many links to other special needs organizations, which you can access through the website at: www.nasen.org.uk/links.

4) Special Needs Kids, an organization for parents and carers of children with special needs has a directory of special needs organizations, which you can access at:

http://special-needs-kids.co.uk/organizations.htm. They have also compiled a list of Disabled Sports Clubs for children, which you can access at:

www.special-needs-kids.co.uk/Disabled-Sports.htm.

5) Kidsguide at: www.kidsguide.co.uk has details of special needs clubs and classes in Manchester, Cheshire, Merseyside and North East Wales for children with disabilities and special needs. To access details, go to the website and select your area followed by 'Clubs and Classes' then 'Disability and special needs sports & clubs'.

Becoming Involved as a Parent

There are lots of opportunities to become involved as a volunteer helper at clubs for children with special needs. Often, these groups are run as charities, and they therefore welcome volunteer help. There is the added advantage that if you are a parent of a child with a particular special need, you will have many of the skills and approaches required to look after other children in a similar situation.

You may need to undergo a CRB check before you can help out. It is best to enquire with the particular club or group to find out if they have any specific requirements.

Chapter 24 - Finding out More

At the end of each chapter we have given resources, if available, to enable you to find out more information about particular types of groups. If you are struggling to find a group in your area to suit your child's particular interests, then the following tips should help.

1) Try entering a search term in the Internet which relates to the particular activity. It is worthwhile trying several combinations of words to see which results show up for each. For example, if your child has an interest in pottery you could try entering, 'children's pottery classes', 'pottery groups', 'pottery clubs' or 'arts and crafts clubs'. There are a couple of useful websites that are a really good source of information regarding children's activities in general. These are: www.kidsguide.co.uk, which also has advice for parents, and:

www.childrensleisure.co.uk.

2) Your local library will have a wealth of information on groups in your area. Most libraries will also allow you to use the Internet if you do not have Internet services available at home.

3) Your local authority is another good source of information and most local authority websites are very detailed. Some allow you to enter a search term, or have an A to Z of services. If you can't find

a website for your local authority, look up their phone number and ring and ask to be put through to the relevant department. You may even find that your local authority publishes regular brochures relating to events and activities in your area. You can find a list of local authorities in the UK at: www.direct.gov.uk/en/Dl1/Directories/Localcouncil s/AToZOfLocalCouncils/index.htm.

4) Children's Centres are located throughout the UK with over 3,600 in England alone. We have already touched on these in some of our previous chapters because of the services for special needs, and because they often run parent and toddler groups and/or playgroups. However, Children's Centres (which you will also hear referred to as Sure Start Centres) also provide a wide range of other services for parents and children so it is worthwhile checking them out.

Some of the services offered at Children's Centres include: health services, parenting advice, dental care, childcare and early learning facilities, help for parents finding work or training opportunities, English language improvement classes, and Citizens' Advice.

Each centre varies in the services it offers although certain services have to be offered by every Children's Centre. You can find your nearest Children's Centre at:

http://childrenscentresfinder.direct.gov.uk/childrens centresfinder/.

5) Check out the following for children's clubs and activities:

Libraries (as mentioned under point 2 above), art galleries, local authority sports centres, schools and colleges, museums, church halls, community centres, stately homes, parks and some farms. NB Some private enterprises also run special schemes for children during school holidays such as private leisure centres' holiday programmes and reduced prices for the cinema or bowling.

6) www.whatson4me.co.uk along with its sister sites:

www.whatson4littleones.co.uk
www.whatson4schoolkids.co.uk
www.whatson4kidsparties.co.uk

give listings of activities and events in different areas of the UK.

You can access the listings on each of these websites by entering your town in the home page, except the whatson4kidsparties website, which enables you to access the listings via an interactive map.

7) You should also find the following resources useful:

- The Pre-school Learning Alliance at: www.pre-school.org.uk. This is a membership organization related to pre-school children. It offers childcare services, family support, and information and advice.
- Under 5s.co.uk at: www.underfives.co.uk supports early years education and gives free advice and resources to teachers and parents with the aim of delivering the Early Years Foundation Stage.

How to Obtain Further Copies

A digital version and a print version of 'Kids' Clubs and Organizations' are both available to purchase through Amazon at:

www.amazon.co.uk/dp/B008IG41DU.

About the Author

Diane Mannion started her writing career 13 years ago when, whilst studying towards her writing diploma, she began to work as a freelance writer, publishing many articles in well-known UK magazines. These included a series of parenting articles for the former 'Mum's Survival Guide' section of Bella magazine. Through contacts she then had the opportunity to work with a web developer as well as producing a series of case studies for Manchester Education Department regarding parental involvement in their children's school life.

As a result of these two opportunities Diane began to put her writing skills to use in other areas. She developed a knowledge and understanding of copywriting techniques and SEO copywriting through attending various courses combined with practical experience.

Since 2007 Diane has operated Diane Mannion Writing Services, a business offering a range of copywriting, editing and proofreading services to businesses and individuals. Diane employs other trusted and skilled freelancers on an ad-hoc basis to help with larger projects.

One of the areas where Diane has gained a great depth of expertise over the years is in ghost writing books on behalf of clients. This is an area of the business that Diane finds particularly rewarding because of the sense of achievement in having completed a lengthy piece of work.

This first book published under the name of Diane Mannion combines her talents in book writing together with experience both as a parent of two teenagers and as a writer of parenting topics. We hope you find this book useful.

You can find out more about Diane Mannion Writing Services at: www.dianemannion.co.uk, or by emailing: dianewriting@googlemail.com. You can also follow Diane on Twitter: @dydywriter, and on Facebook at:

http://www.facebook.com/pages/Diane-Mannion-Writing-Services/285019144850839. Please feel free to let us have feedback regarding the book via our Facebook page.

Also by Diane Mannion

Non-Fiction

The next non-fiction book to be released by Diane Mannion will be:

Great Locations for Kids' Parties

Give your child a birthday party to remember by having it at one of his favourite settings such as a cinema or zoo! We have scoured the UK to find top locations for you to stage the ultimate kids' birthday party. As well as traditional venues that host children's parties we've covered lots of places that you might not have thought of.

We know that organizing a sensational children's party can be a demanding and stressful time for parents. There are so many things to think about:

How do you get to the venue?

How many children can you invite?

What about the cake?

What type of food does the venue serve?

Is there anything you need to bring?

…and so on.

That's why we've organized every chapter of the book into informative sections covering aspects such as: finding these types of venues, approximate costs, what is included in the cost, suitable ages, and whether the venue has any specific requirements in terms of the number of children, food etc.

Each chapter of the book is based on a particular type of location or activity and is packed full of useful facts and advice. By arming yourself with this information you can ensure that you are well prepared. This will enable you to have a stress-free party allowing you to relax and enjoy watching the kids have fun. After all, why party at home when you can let someone-else take care of everything? As well as taking the pressure off you, this book provides a valuable source of inspiration.

Great ideas for great parties!

Find out More - To find out up-to-date news regarding release dates and where to purchase a copy please refer to our website at: www.dianemannion.co.uk. You can also find updates on the Diane Mannion author page at Amazon, on our Twitter feed at: @dydywriter and on our Facebook page at:

http://www.facebook.com/pages/Diane-Mannion-Writing-Services/285019144850839.

Fiction

Diane's first novel is scheduled for release in 2013:

Slur

Julie Quinley is a young woman with everything to live for – a good job, a loving family, an active social life and a doting boyfriend, Vinny. Unfortunately, however, the dramatic events of one fateful night are about to change the course of her existence forever.

When one of Julie's workmates dies of a drink and drugs overdose, Julie and her best friend Rita are wrongly accused of the killing. Julie has to bear the slights and accusations of her office colleagues and life becomes unbearable. The pressure seeps through to her personal life, and, believing that she has lost the respect of her close family and friends, Julie sinks into a pit of despair. Unknown to Julie, however, they are rallying to her support.

Julie reaches a turning point when Rita reveals that Vinny has found out who the killer really is. Realising that she must act in order to clear her name, Julie joins Vinny and Rita in trying to find evidence against their suspect.

Proving a vicious murderer guilty, however, is never going to be easy, especially when the police remain convinced that Julie and Rita are the culprits. After several daring but thwarted attempts at entrapping their suspect, Julie and her friends hire a private detective. Eventually they find the evidence they need and await the trial.

But is he really the killer? A shock discovery in court adds a final twist to the story.

This crime thriller is enriched by a strong interplay of characters throughout. The girls have very colourful personalities and the electrifying atmosphere surrounding them is fully brought to life.

<u>Find out More</u> - A digital version of this book will be available soon. Please view the website: <u>www.dianemannion.co.uk</u> for news of release dates. You can also visit the Diane Mannion author page at Amazon, or find updates on our Twitter feed at: @dydywriter and on our Facebook page at:

<u>http://www.facebook.com/pages/Diane-Mannion-Writing-Services/285019144850839</u>.

Disclaimer

The information contained in this book results from extensive research carried out by the author and does not in any way represent an endorsement of any of the services offered by the organizations named in the book. All prices and other facts are based on information obtained through research, and were correct at the time of compilation. However, it is possible that some of the information, or websites referred to in this book, may have changed since the book was compiled. The author accepts no responsibility for any dealings that you may have with any of the named organizations or with other children's organizations, clubs or groups.
